# Art of the Needle

## 100 Masterpiece Quilts
## from the Shelburne Museum

by Henry Joyce

Research Assistant
Martha Strum

*Shelburne Museum*
*Shelburne, Vermont*

© 2003 Shelburne Museum, Inc.
Second printing.
All rights reserved. Printed in Canada.


*Cover:*
Detail of *Crazy Patchwork Quilt* (2003-2), see page 126.


ISBN: 0-939384-27-2


*Graphic Design*
Vicky McCafferty


*Printed By*
Transcontinental Printing, Lachine, Quebec


*Published By*
Shelburne Museum, U.S. Route 7, P.O. Box 10, Shelburne, Vermont 05482

# Table *of* Contents

# Acknowledgements

*by Hope Alswang*
*President, Shelburne Museum*

All exhibitions are the product of many people. The exhibition that this publication accompanies, *Art of the Needle: 100 Masterpiece Quilts from the Shelburne Museum,* is no exception. The creativity and dedication of many staff members and volunteers, past and present, made this major project possible. Each department has been involved with this undertaking — in some cases, over several years.

I want to acknowledge two former Shelburne Museum employees whose commitment to the quilt collection is the foundation of this major exhibition. Lilian Baker Carlisle's scholarship first "decoded" these wonderful objects, and Celia Oliver's involvement with the collection insured its visibility over the years.

All Shelburne Museum collections benefit from the thoughtful, skilled work of the Conservation Department under the direction of Richard Kerschner. Conservator Nancie Ravenel worked to ensure that these fragile objects are both accessible and beautiful. Many dedicated conservation volunteers helped in the effort: Jill Aiken, Marjorie Allard, Joyce Dawson, Pat DiSilvio, Nancy Ewen, Jeanne LaPlante, Linda Jackson Lees (who also reorganized the catalogue notebooks), Bernice McAteer, and Gloria McEwen.

Associate registrar Barbara Rathburn's knowledge of the collection and remarkable memory has been an asset to this project.

Particular thanks go to the Buildings and Grounds Department staff, who solved countless problems while preparing for this exhibition. Their fine craftsmanship is evident throughout the installation. Thanks to director Bob Furrer, Loren Cox, David Furlong, Rick Gage, Donna Kennedy, Chris Kent, Jon Kent, Tony Pinard-Brace, Brian Pornelos, Chip Stulen, and faithful volunteer John Boyden. Special thanks to Bob Titemore, who designed an inventive batten system that increases display space for quilts and will benefit visitors for years to come.

Chief curator Henry Joyce led this project, and his fine eye has created a wonderful exhibition. Librarian/archivist Polly Darnell provided research assistance, and curatorial assistant Martha Strum's research and general help throughout the project were invaluable. Exhibit preparator Douglas Oaks was involved with the project from its inception, and his contributions to this exhibition have been significant. Public programs coordinator Jen Mitiguy provided wonderful educational content and visitor perspective in the development of the exhibition. Over the last three years, Amelia Peck, associate curator in the Department of American Decorative Arts at The Metropolitan Museum of Art, has been a valued consultant.

This book is a testament to the considerable talents of graphic designer Vicky McCafferty, who imbues her work with charm and liveliness.

Chairman of the Board Philip R. von Stade and the Board of Trustees offered support throughout the planning for this exhibition as they do for all projects at Shelburne Museum. The staff is so grateful for their commitment and enthusiasm.

*Detail of Horse and Birds Album Quilt (10-15), see page 46.*

# Introduction

Shelburne Museum in Shelburne, Vermont has one of the largest and best-quality bedcover collections in the United States. This book highlights 100 masterpiece quilts, most of them made between 1800 and 1900, from this extraordinary collection. Publication coincides with the Museum's largest-ever quilt exhibition, *Art of the Needle: 100 Masterpiece Quilts from the Shelburne Museum* ( May 17 - October 26, 2003).

*Green Whole-Cloth Quilt (10-156), see page 32.*

Art of the Needle

*Shelburne Museum founder Electra Havemeyer Webb at the Museum, about 1955.*

The richness and diversity of these quilts is a testament to Museum founder Electra Havemeyer Webb's trailblazing vision and passion for collecting. Mrs. Webb was an eclectic, encyclopedic, and influential early collector of American art and artifacts, and she donated to the Museum dozens of quilts that she had amassed since the 1920s.

When Shelburne Museum first opened in 1952, quilts were exhibited solely as decorative accessories in historic house settings. But Mrs. Webb made Shelburne the country's first museum to formally showcase quilts as works of art when, in 1954, she moved a barn to the grounds and created within it unique gallery spaces for textiles. This gallery held America's first major collection of quilts on public view.

Throughout the history of quilt-making, the finest pieces have been made to be admired rather than used. Quilts were highly prized as works of art and were brought out of cupboards or trunks only on special occasions. By the mid-19th century, there were increasing public venues for their display, including state and county fairs, where quilt-makers competed for prizes.

The first quilts in America that came from England were whole-cloth. Two from the late 18th or early 19th century are included here. One of them, the calimanco (glazed wool) *Green Whole-Cloth Quilt* (10-156), uses a color linked with Venus, the Roman goddess of love and beauty, since the Renaissance. Green had been widely used for textiles on fabulous royal beds, where the issue of fertility was of supreme importance.

*Stars and Pinwheel Medallion Quilt (10-283), see page 69.*

In the 19th century, nearly all American women faced the everyday task of sewing. Even women with dressmakers made their own "home" dresses as well as children's and servants' clothing and men's shirts. It was generally believed that the repetition of needlework taught women the virtues of patience and gentility. Although the sewing machine was invented in the late 1840s, models were not generally available in homes until after the Civil War. Even then, sewing machines were rarely used in fine quilt-making before the 20th century.

Instruction in the art of quilting and embroidery began at an early age, and in some communities it was common for a girl to have completed her first quilt by the age of five. An example of a child-made quilt from the Museum's collection is the *Stars and Pinwheel Medallion Quilt* (10-283), made by Sarah Johnson (1812-1876) of Pennsylvania when she was 14. This quilt has more than 50 different fabrics and displays the young woman's remarkably accomplished needlework.

By the time of her marriage, a young woman had often produced a group of quilts for her dowry. The *Lily Flower Quilt* (10-732) on p.59, for example, is inscribed in pen *No. 6 M.B.*, probably indicating that this was the sixth quilt that maker Mary Beaman stitched before her wedding in 1851. One of the stars of Shelburne's collection is the recently acquired Ohio-made *Catherine Williams Quilt* (2001-24) that probably celebrates the 1871 marriage of Baltimore-born Catherine Cox to Newton Allen Williams, whose name is embroidered on the front along with the date 1873. It might easily have taken two years to finish such richly detailed narrative scenes and decorative blocks.

Quilt-making also was an expression of commitment to a wider community. This book includes several friendship quilts, including *Floral Album Quilt* (10-151), probably made in Virginia. It bears longhand inscriptions on most of its blocks with such messages as *To mother 1854* and *Mother to Sue 1855*. It is an exceptionally grand bedcover made from expensive glazed chintzes in brilliant colors, and it is in excellent condition. Another friendship quilt from the south is *Floral Friendship Quilt* (10-292) on p.47, made in 1847 by women whose names are inscribed in longhand.

*Catherine Williams Quilt (2001-24), see page 40.*

*Floral Album Quilt (10-151), see page 19.*

*Odd Fellows Album Quilt (10-141), see page 42.*

*Pheasant and Mandarin Duck Motif Whole-Cloth Quilt (10-725), see page 30.*

A natural extension of women's devotion to family and friends was their participation in charity work. Women often headed benevolent and missionary societies that raised money for good causes. An illustration of this is *Odd Fellows Album Quilt* (10-141), won by Dr. M.H. Bixby at a post-Civil War fund-raising bazaar. The magnificent quilt is decorated with several Odd Fellows symbols, including the image of a heart in the palm of a hand that reminds members to be open to (and concerned for) others. Another Baltimore album quilt of extraordinary quality is the 1846 *Major Ringgold Quilt* (10-330) on p.44, made with solid colors and abstract-patterned cotton typical of the mid-19th century. Major Ringgold, the military hero commemorated in the quilt, died that year in the Mexican-American War. Elaborately worked quilts like this one were made with expensive new fabrics and took thousands of hours to complete.

Among the 100 masterpieces are a dozen signed in ink or embroidery by their makers. Clearly, the quilters valued their work and wanted their names to be remembered. One of the earliest signed quilts is the *Pheasant and Mandarin Duck Motif Whole-Cloth Quilt* (10-725) from New York, marked in ink *Susan Woolley 1810.* Probably the best signed appliquéd piece in the collection is the *Diamond Medallion Quilt Top* (10-327), marked *Mary Jane Carr's/ Quilt completed in/1854.* Family oral histories attribute makers to about 25 of the quilts, but nearly two-thirds of the 100 pieces have no record of their makers.

*Diamond Medallion Quilt Top (10-327), see page 55.*

*Botanical Quilt (10-323), see page 54.*

Appliquéd and pieced quilts represent the largest groups here. The appliqués include a range of traditional designs, such as lotus flower, rose, double tulip, laurel leaf, lily, pine tree, and oak leaf patterns. There are also original designs from different parts of the country. One of the most charming is *Botanical Quilt* (10-323) from Pennsylvania from about 1850, which has the names of flowers stitched below the designs. Also from Pennsylvania is the remarkable 1830s *Flower Basket Bedcover* in reverse appliqué (10-271), a relatively rare technique that demands advanced sewing skills. One of the most beautiful and unusual pieces in this section is the late 19th-century *Sunflower Quilt* (10-651) on p.61, made by Carrie M.

*Detail of Flower Basket Bedcover (10-271), see page 57.*

Carpenter of Northfield, Vermont. Although some might describe it as a provincial piece, the quilt is in the highly sophisticated style of the Arts and Crafts Movement, in which the sunflower was a central part of the style vocabulary. The quilt is both magnificent in its design and exceptional in its needlework.

The pieced quilts include geometrically based patterns such as the *Pincushion Quilt* (10-164) on p.89, the bold *Hexagons and Triangles Quilt* (10-338) on p. 94, the *Mariner's Compass Quilt* (10-22) on p.97, and the glorious *Lesson in Geometry Quilt* (10-334) on p.85, which relies on only two colors (pumpkin-orange and white) to make a stunning visual effect. Also in this section are log cabin quilts, including the powerful *Windmill Blades Quilt* (10-133) on p.106.

Amish and Mennonite quilts are some of the most visually dramatic quilts ever made. The most striking example here is the Amish *Concentric Squares Quilt* (10-671) from Lancaster County, Pennsylvania. The quilt's slate blue and red fabrics pulsate with energy and excitement in the same way that Op Art paintings of the 1960s had colors jumping off the surface of the canvas. The fine Amish *Double Nine-Patch Quilt* (10-667) is from the Midwest.

Among crazy quilts, the most original by far are two quilts made in the 1870s by members of the Haskins family of Rochester, Vermont. The wonderful images in these cotton quilts (including blackbirds, cats, squirrels, a mother and child, and a man playing a violin) demonstrate

*Concentric Squares Quilt (10-671), see page 119.*

*Double Nine-Patch Quilt (10-667), see page 116.*

*Haskins Quilt (2003-2), see page 126.*

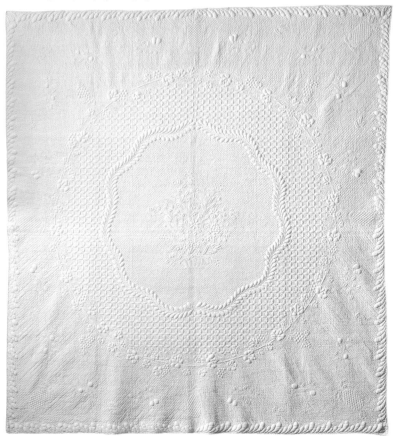

*Floral Wreath Whitework Quilt (10-43), see page 135.*

an unusual imaginative freedom. The pieces were made about a decade before crazy quilts became popular and kits (complete with pre-cut silks and velvets and machine-embroidered flowers) became widely available.

In contrast to the rich textures and colors of the crazy quilts, white-on-white bedcovers convey a mood of serenity and calm. *Floral Wreath Whitework Quilt* (10-43) is beautifully quilted with a large, undulating framework of exquisite needlework. *Sailing Ships Whitework Quilt* (10-21) on p.138 from Mass-achusetts features sloop-rigged sailing vessels that rest on quilted waves with gulls soaring and gliding in the white muslin sky above.

Shelburne Museum continues to acquire significant American quilts. The most recent examples include a crazy quilt on p. 126 given to the Museum in February 2003 by Henry Haskins Pierce, Jr. and a baby quilt, *Scenes of Childhood Crib Quilt* (2002-37) on p.52, which was bought at auction in October 2002. Made about 1872, its images of children are taken from books and magazines of the time. The quilt matches a pillow sham by the same unidentified maker already at the Museum and is a stunning addition to Shelburne's appliquéd quilts. Today, Shelburne Museum's quilts and textiles collection spans three centuries and is known internation-ally for its exceptional depth, range, and quality.

*Detail of Scenes of Childhood Crib Quilt (2002-37), see page 52.*

# Chintz Appliquéd Quilts

These quilts feature illusionistic flower-printed cottons known as chintz (from the Hindi word *chitta*, meaning spotted). The first European-made copperplate chintzes, with their large, flamboyant floral prints based on traditional South Asian patterns, were introduced to America from England in the 18th century. Chintz fabrics were extremely expensive, and by cutting pieces to appliqué on a quilt, a small amount of costly fabric could be used to provide a design for a much larger surface. Only well-to-do women could afford the fabrics and had the leisure time to make chintz appliquéd quilts.

*Detail of Tree of Life Bedcover (10-93), see page 20.*

**Attributed to a member of the Ridgley family**

*Chintz Floral Quilt*
Baltimore, Maryland
Early 19th century
Printed, appliquéd, and quilted
cotton
108" x 80"
Museum purchase, 1954
10-145 (1954-492)

The flowers, which include lilies and roses, have been cut from high-quality European-made chintzes. The flower sprays in the two central blocks have been painstakingly appliquéd with densely sewn stitches that give these blocks stronger visual prominence than the ten surrounding them. Another fine feature is the quilted white ground of each block, including scrolling branches that shadow the flowing forms of the polychrome flowers.

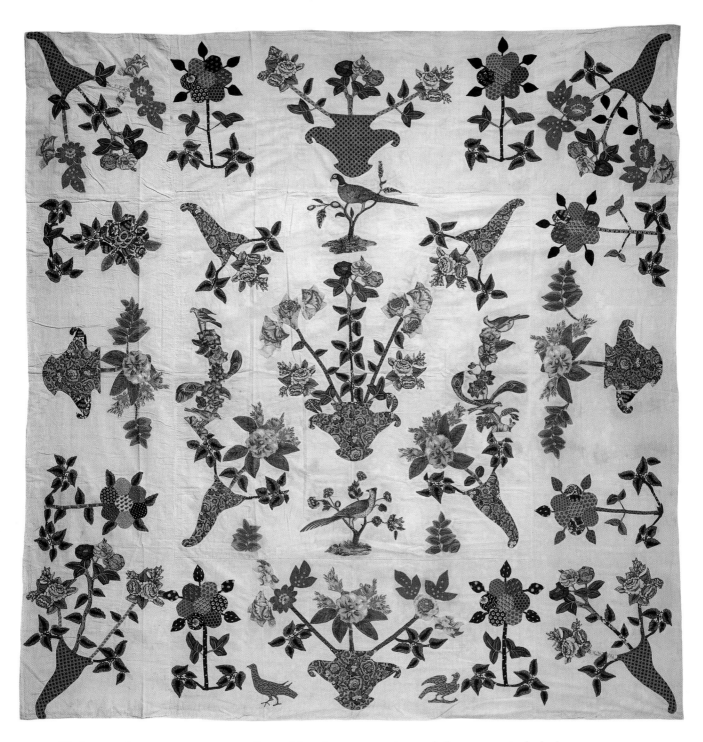

**Maker unknown**

*Cornucopias and Flowers Bedcover*

Probably New England

Early 19th century

Printed and appliquéd cotton and
linen; unquilted

100" x 100"

Gift of Electra Havemeyer Webb,
1952

10-29 (1952-552)

By making the cornucopias and flowers particularly large, a conventional neoclassical vocabulary has been transformed into a magnificent design statement. The maker created an additional visual dynamic by contrasting large shapes (note the finely printed birds) with others that are quite small (as in the chintz flowers used for the bodies of several vases). The wide border includes eight bold patchwork flowers made from more than a dozen differently patterned fabrics.

Art of the Needle

**Maker unknown**

*Chintz Flowers and Animals Bedcover*

Probably New England

Early 19th century

Printed, appliquéd, and embroidered
cotton; unquilted

94" x 91"

Gift of Electra Havemeyer Webb,
1952

10-54 (1952-577)

The floral-printed textiles have been cleverly manipulated to suggest the colors and shading of fur and feathers of foxes, squirrels, and birds. Other exceptional animal images worked in the same way include dogs, cats, cows, and horses. By contrast, the clusters of flowers are rather conventionally designed. All of the appliqués have been sewn with a button-hole stitch. The nine octagon-shaped reserves and all of the quilt edges have been made from binding tape or braid that was hand-woven on a small braid loom.

**Attributed to Sibyl Spaulding or Lydia Cadwick Spaulding**

*Octagon Appliquéd Bedcover*
American or British
Early 19th century
Printed, pieced, and appliquéd cotton and linen; unquilted
83" x 96"
Museum purchase, 1957
10-242 (1957-533)

The piece was once owned by Roland Harty Spaulding, who was governor of New Hampshire in 1915-16. He suggested it was made either by his great-grandmother Sibyl or his grandmother Lydia.

The top's design, using octagonal- and diamond-shaped reserves, is distinctive of the early 19th-century neoclassical style. The printed appliquéd images, some of which commemorate the British capture of Gibraltar in 1782, are cut from the very best-quality English textiles. This work is highly sophisticated in both concept and craftsmanship.

**Members of the
Townsend, Fuller, Pope,
and Mikell families**

*Floral Chintz Album Bedcover*

Possibly Virginia

1850-57

Printed, pieced, and appliquéd
cotton; unquilted

112" x 109"

Museum purchase, 1954

10-151 (1954-412)

Fifteen of the blocks bear longhand inscriptions in pen. Among them
are *Mary E. Townsend, I. Jenkins Mikell 1850, Susan E. Fuller February
1857, Mary K. Pope, To Mother 1854,* and *My God I would not doubt
Thy wisdom or Thy grace.* It is likely the bedcover was a present. Family
history held that it came from an unidentified Virginia plantation.

This exceptionally grand bedcover was made from expensive glazed
chintzes in brilliant colors and is still in excellent condition. The
piece's floral design is based on late 18th-century high-style French
textiles that were revived in the 1850s, both in Europe and America.
These fabrics probably were manufactured in England.

**Maker unknown**

*Tree of Life Bedcover with Vases, Birds, and Pineapples*

Probably New England

Early 19th century

Printed and appliquéd English-made cotton and linen; unquilted

106" x 103"

Gift of Electra Havemeyer Webb, 1952

10-93 (1952-613)

The maker cut a wide range of English-made chintzes to create branches, flowers, leaves, and birds. Throughout the piece, images are combined with flat-patterned fabrics (note the dark green leaves of the central tree). The bedcover pays homage to the traditional tree of life design that was first used on European bed-furnishing textiles adapted from South Asian prototypes as early as the 16th century.

**Maker unknown**

*Tree of Life Bedcover*

Probably Southern U.S.

Mid 19th century

Printed and appliquéd cotton;

unquilted

106" x 100"

Purchased from John K. Byard, 1957

10-236

The quilt is similar in overall design to several examples from Virginia and North and South Carolina that use the tree of life motif inside a scalloped medallion. In comparison to the bedcover opposite, this one appears more conventional and lacks the other's highly individual character.

**Maker unknown**

*Chinoiserie Bedcover*

American or British

Early 19th century

Printed English cottons appliquéd to a diamond-patterned woven ground and embroidered; unquilted

95" x 97"

Purchased from Elinor Merrell, New York City, 1958

10-310 (1958-225)

The ambitious maker of this bedcover used a multitude of printed fabrics to create unusual landscape and garden scenes. Two of the most prominent were inspired by Chinese art as interpreted in 18th-century European design manuals such as *Livres de chinoise (A New Book of Chinese Ornaments)* by Jean Pillement, London, 1758.

In this bedcover's most intricate scene, a woman with embroidered features sits at a dressing table adjusting her headdress, while across from her a gentleman sits playing a stringed instrument. The combination of elaborate design and fine craftsmanship make this a remarkable piece.

**Attributed to**
**Martha Custis Peter**
**(1777-1854)**

*Flowers and Fruit Baskets Quilt*

American

Early 19th century

Printed, glazed, appliquéd, and
quilted cotton

103" x 98"

Museum purchase, 1953

10-116 (1953-1117)

In the center of this magnificent quilt is an impos-
ing magnolia blossom surrounded by clusters of
flowers and baskets of fruit. Its probable maker,
Martha Custis Peter, was the granddaughter of
Martha Custis Washington, George Washington's
wife. Another quilt, preserved at the Peter family
house (Tudor Place in Georgetown, Washington
D.C.) is made with some of the same printed cottons.

*Martha Custis Peter, painted about 1785 by Armistead Peter III*
*(1896-1983). (Photo courtesy of Tudor Place.)*

**Florence Cowdin Peto
(1880-1970)**

*Calico Garden Crib Quilt*

Tenafly, New Jersey

1950

Pieced, appliquéd, and quilted

cotton

49" x 39"

Museum purchase, 1952

10-25 (1952-548)

This crib-size quilt was made from a variety of 18th- and 19th-century fabrics: hand-blocked and copperplate prints, chintzes, and other English and French cottons.

Florence Peto first collected and researched quilts as a hobby, but it soon developed into a professional pursuit. She lectured to quilt groups, wrote magazine articles, and published two books on quilts. She helped Shelburne Museum founder Electra Havemeyer Webb acquire and catalogue many quilts in the Museum's collection. It was Mrs. Peto's passionate collecting and research that led her to make quilts as well. This is a charming example of the colonial revival style.

**Ann Robinson**

*Floral Medallion Bedcover*

New England, possibly Connecticut

1814

Stitched *Ann Robinson October 1 1813*

and *Finished January 27 1814*

Pieced and appliquéd printed cotton

100" x 95"

Purchased from John K. Byard, 1954

10-140 (1954-439)

This transitional piece illustrates the emerging style of 19th-century appliquéd quilts that eventually use no chintzes. While many American quilts at this time were made with chintzes predominating, the only chintz is this quilt is used for the red birds in the bottom section. The trees, cornucopia, and bouquets of flowers are made with newer-style, flat patterned fabrics, but their shapes are strongly neoclassical.

Ann Robinson
October 1st
1813 ~

# Whole-Cloth Quilts

Whole-cloth quilts are made from yardage of manufactured wool cloth (calimanco, usually produced in England) or from widths of cotton cloth printed with patterns (also usually English made).

These whole-cloth quilts date mainly from the late 18th century to the middle of the 19th century.

*Detail of The Dance and The Departure Whole-Cloth Quilt, see page 34.*

**Susannah Rebecca Woolley (1786-1880)**

*Pheasant and Mandarin Duck Motif Whole-Cloth Quilt*

Kings Point, Long Island, New York

Cross-stitched on the back *Susan Woolley 1810*

Quilted copperplate printed cotton

90" x 86"

Gift of Mrs. Gordon Smith, 1993

10-725 (1993-14)

This English bird print, first made about 1780, was still in production in the early 19th century. Designs with birds were particularly prevalent in English cottons until about 1820. Many examples survive in America, suggesting that they were exported after the War of 1812 as the British flooded the American market with printed cottons in an effort to stifle the young country's textile industry.

**Melinda Brown or her daughter, Marietta Scribner**

*Green Whole-Cloth Quilt*
Corinth, Vermont
Late 18th or early 19th century
Quilted English calimanco
94½" x 90"
Purchased from Mrs. George Taylor, 1955
10-156 (1955-617)

Calimanco was glazed all-wool fabric manufactured in England, primarily for use in clothing. For this bedcover, plain calimanco was quilted with a neoclassical scrolling pattern typical of the period.

Shelburne Museum bought the quilt from Mrs. George Taylor, a great-granddaughter of Melinda Brown.

**Maker unknown**

*Red Whole-Cloth Quilt*

American or British

Late 18th or early 19th century

Quilted English calimanco

96" x 100"

Museum purchase, 1954

10-196 (1954-539.2)

Plain-weave calimanco quilts in solid colors are regularly found in American collections. This one shows little evidence of wear and is in excellent condition. The quilting may have been done in this country, but ready-made quilts of this sort also were exported from England to the United States.

**Attributed to a member of the Dutton family of Wilmington, Connecticut**

*The Dance and The Departure Whole-Cloth Quilt, 1815-20*

Roller-printed and quilted cotton with linen backing, 90" x 76"

Gift of Mrs. Charles E. Wilson in memory of her father Frank Jenkins, 1954

10-131 (1954-67)

The two scenes, *The Dance* and *The Departure,* are based on late 18th-century illustrations of Oliver Goldsmith's poem "The Deserted Village," published in 1770. This English roller-printed textile is attributed to the Manchester printworks of John Marshall and is based on a better-quality copperplate-printed version of the same scenes from about 1795.

The quilt was a gift to the Museum from a descendent of the Dutton family of Wilmington, Connecticut.

**Maker unknown**

*Riverside Temple Whole-Cloth Quilt*
Probably Starksboro, Vermont
Mid 19th century
Roller-printed, glazed, and quilted
cotton
89" x 96"
Museum purchase, 1955
10-168 (1955-646)

Because the green and brown in this quilt are not commonly found in English-printed cottons, the fabric is thought to be American-made. The subject, too, may be American — probably a landscape garden overlooking the Hudson River somewhere between New York City and Albany.

According to Museum records, a letter from the last private owner states, "This quilt was made and placed in the Hope chest of a woman who was married in 1821 ... She lived her life in Starksboro, Vermont."

**Attributed to Abigail Livermore Keyes of Wilton, New Hampshire**

*Feather-Vine Whole-Cloth Quilt*
Late 18th century
Quilted English calimanco
104" x 98"
Museum purchase, 1987
10-656 (1987-38)

Family tradition holds that Abigail Livermore Keyes (1721-1801) made this quilt for her brother, the Rev. Jonathon Livermore, on the occasion of his marriage in 1769. It is also said that Rev. Livermore drew the quilting design for Abigail. The piece was passed down through the family to the last private owner, who still lived in Rev. Livermore's Wilton homestead when he sold the quilt to the Museum. Whole-cloth quilts in this style were made throughout the late 18th and early 19th centuries in both England and America. This one is reversible; it is quilted on the back in the same design, but in lavender.

# Album Quilts

True album quilts are made of blocks sewn by different women who usually signed their work. Only two bedcovers in this section (10-15 and 10-292) are album quilts in that sense, but the other four share the album vocabulary of 16 to 36 equal-sized square blocks and the prominent use of fashionable red and green fabrics. Common motifs in the album patterns include wreaths, flowers, and fruit. These themes reflect the influence of the rococo and neoclassical revival styles. Most appliqué work on Baltimore album quilts was done with the relatively invisible stitch still used today. The finest of the group is the *Major Ringgold Album Quilt.* Like all quilts of this type, it is made of expensive fabrics rather than scraps and has virtually no batting (which indicates that it was never intended for use). The quilt shows no sign of wear and probably has never been washed.

*Detail of Floral Friendship Quilt (10-292), see page 47.*

**Catherine Cox Williams**

*Album Quilt*

Probably made in Ohio

Dated 1873

Pieced, appliquéd, and embroidered

cotton, linen, and silk

93³/₄" x 93⁵/₈"

Museum purchase, 2001

2001-24

This unusual design is dominated by figural blocks depicting scenes from the life of the quilt's maker and owner. The Conestoga wagon near the center is embroidered with the inscription *N.A. Williams, 1873*. According to family history, the quilt commemorates the 1871 marriage of Newton Allen Williams (who as a boy had traveled overland with his father to Oregon) and Catherine Cox (who was probably from Baltimore). It is likely that Catherine made the quilt for her husband.

The flowers and wreaths owe a considerable debt to the Baltimore album style of the 1840s and '50s. This quilt, though, with its many narrative scenes and rare African American figures, breaks the conventions of the earlier, more purely decorative Baltimore style.

**Maker unknown**

*Odd Fellows Album Quilt*

Probably Baltimore, Maryland

About 1850

Appliquéd and quilted stuffed cotton and velvet

112" x 112"

Museum purchase, 1954

10-141 (1954-429)

The quilt's design is consistent with Baltimore-made album quilts of the mid 19th century. The block at the top left depicts Baltimore's Washington Monument, completed in 1829.

On the back is a longhand inscription in ink: *Property of Mrs. E. Merle Bixby, 43 Hollis Street, Providence, Rhode Island*. The quilt was said to have been won by Mrs. Bixby's husband at a post-Civil War bazaar organized by the Providence Lodge of the Independent Order of the Odd Fellows to raise money for welfare work. The Odd Fellows, a benevolent organization, originated in late 18th-century England, and the first lodge in America was established about 1819 in Baltimore.

*The heart in a hand was used by the Independent Order of the Odd Fellows to symbolize members' openness to others. At the top of the square, the all-seeing eye reminds members of God's all-knowing power.*

**Maker unknown**

*Major Ringgold Album Quilt*

Baltimore, Maryland

1846

Pieced and appliquéd quilted cotton

94" x 110"

Purchased from E. Haydon Parks,

1959

10-330

The quilt's design is distinctive of the finest Baltimore album quilts. The top center block depicts the temporary memorial erected in 1846 to honor Major Samuel Ringgold. Major Ringgold was born in 1800 in Washington County, Maryland and died a hero in the battle of Palo Alto on May 11, 1846 during the Mexican-American War. A Currier and Ives print commemorating the battle and his death was published that same year.

**Made by a member of the Hundloser family**

*Horse and Birds Album Quilt*

Maryland

Mid 19th century

Pieced, appliquéd, and quilted

cotton

98" x 101"

Purchased from Florence Cowdin

Peto, 1952

10-15 (1952-538)

The quilt's design and colors are close in style to Baltimore album quilts of the 1840s and '50s, but its blocks are less refined. This is one of many quilts that Shelburne Museum founder Electra Havemeyer Webb bought from Florence Cowdin Peto (1880-1970). Mrs. Peto was perhaps the most influential force promoting quilt-making and quilt scholarship in the first half of the 20th century.

Margaret Head,
Elizabeth Miller, and
others
*Floral Friendship Quilt*
Baltimore, Maryland
Marked in ink *Margaret Head,*
*Elizabeth Miller,* and *S. A. Mules*
Dated 1847
Pieced, appliquéd, embroidered,
and quilted cotton
102" x 100"
Museum purchase, 1958
10-292 (1958-143)

The design and execution of this quilt are similar to those in a group preserved at the Maryland Historical Society. Those are attributed to an as-yet-unidentified designer of decorative squares known as "Designer II." Her work uses the traditional red and green color scheme and flowers made of ruched tape, as seen in the bottom center square of this quilt.

**Attributed to Minnie Burdick**

*Centennial Album Quilt*

North Adams, Massachusetts

1876

Pieced and appliquéd cotton

79" x 78"

Museum purchase, 1987

10-653 (1987-40)

Very little is recorded about Minnie Burdick except that she married Herbert Childs of North Adams, Massachusetts in 1877. The quilt remained in the Burdick-Childs family until shortly before its purchase by Shelburne Museum. Two of the quilt blocks depict buildings from the 1876 Centennial Exhibition held in Philadelphia. One block shows the Agricultural Hall framed with a banner that reads *Declaration of Independence ... Centennial Anniversary ... 1776 ... 1876*. Another depicts the Women's Pavilion.

# Appliquéd Quilts

The quilts in this section date mainly from about 1840 to 1900, when most of the best American appliquéd quilts were made. Improving economic conditions for a growing middle class gave many women more time for fancy needlework.

In appliqué, individual motifs are cut from different fabrics, laid on a usually solid background fabric, and sewn down. Flat patterns of flowers are the predominant decorative vocabulary of appliqué quilts — very different from the illusionistic effect of chintz flowers.

Illustrated books on flowers were widely published in 19th-century America, and women's periodicals regularly published articles on flowers. In the mid century, *Godey's Lady's Book* featured a wildflower of the month and published articles on sketching from nature. The symbolism of flowers was widely and variously interpreted; for example, roses might mean one thing to one person and something else to another. It is virtually impossible to reconstruct the symbolic meanings of flowers on quilts from 100 or more years ago.

*Detail of Diamond Medallion Quilt (10-327), see page 55.*

**Maker unknown**

*Scenes of Childhood Crib Quilt*

Probably New York

About 1872

Appliquéd and embroidered printed
cotton and drawing in ink

38" x 35"

Museum purchase, 2002

2002-37

The appliquéd image at the bottom of this quilt, marked *Dolly is sick*, shows a boy dressed as an adult. The scene is based on an image published in *Peterson's Magazine* in April 1872. The other two vignettes have the following inscriptions: *Here's some more sins in my pocket* and *Gran-Pa ride first*. Note that the faces and hair are drawn in ink.

The Museum acquired this rare quilt in 2002 because it was made by the same unidentified quilter who created a pillow sham (see next page) that has been part of Shelburne's collection since 1954.

*front*

*back*

**Maker unknown**

*Pillow Cover*

Probably New York

Late 19th century

Appliquéd and embroidered printed

cotton and drawing in ink

16¹/₂" x 24"

Gift of Mrs. G.W. Whichelow, 1954

8.1-24 (1954-488)

The pillow cover was appliquéd by the same person who made the *Scenes of Childhood Crib Quilt* (2002-37) on page 52. They share inscriptions, fabrics, and a closely related decorative style.

**Maker unknown**

*Botanical Quilt*

Probably Pennsylvania

About 1850

Appliquéd and quilted cotton

92" x 90½"

Museum purchase

10-323

Stylized flowers and colors restricted to only red and green are characteristic of quilts from the mid-Atlantic states (and particularly Pennsylvania). Note that the names identifying each of the plants are stitched alongside; they include *Hop Vine, Wood Bine* and *Poke Berries*.

**Mary Jane Carr**

*Diamond Medallion Quilt Top*

By tradition from Columbia,
Lancaster County, Pennsylvania

Embroidered *Mary Jane Carr's /
Quilt completed in / 1854*

Appliquéd and embroidered cotton;
unquilted

99" x 92"

Purchased from Elizabeth Spangler,
Ephrata, Pennsylvania, 1959

10-327

Because of its rich pictorial and decorative vocabulary, this is one of the star bedcovers in the Museum's collection.

Mary Jane Carr (b. 1790) incorporated a variety of techniques to create trees, flowers, and animals which, combined with the appliqués, make a richly textured surface. Although the landscapes are not typical of Baltimore quilts in the 1840s and '50s, the flower vases and wreaths are close to the Baltimore style. Columbia, Pennsylvania, where this is said to have been made, is only 20 miles from the Maryland border, and it is reasonable to speculate that Mary Jane Carr might have seen Baltimore quilts and been inspired by them.

**Hannah E. Hamblin Delano (b. 1824)**

*Tree of Life Bedcover*

Bridport, Vermont

Mid 19th century

Appliquéd and embroidered cotton; unquilted

92" x 88"

Museum purchase, 1994

10-741 (1994-42)

The same green fabric used in the tree, wreath, and border give the piece a unified design, while the red flowers and orange fruit bring a vibrant visual interest to the quilt's overall effect.

The tree of life motif is an ancient textile design associated with beds. It was first used by the Europeans in the late 16th century; they were influenced by South Asian textiles that were imported at that time.

Hannah Hamblin was born in 1824 in Bridport, Vermont (about an hour south of Shelburne). In 1847, she married farmer Nelson Delano, and they lived in neighboring Shoreham.

**Maker unknown**

*Flower Basket Bedcover*

Probably Pennsylvania

Mid 19th century

Reverse appliquéd cotton; unquilted

76" x 76"

Museum purchase, 1958

10-271 (1958-41)

The bedcover is worked in reverse appliqué, a relatively rare technique that demands advanced sewing skills. For this piece, the pattern was drawn on the white cotton field, which was then cut away and laid over sections of colored fabrics. The maker then turned under the cut edges of the white cotton and hemmed them to the patterned fabrics below.

**Maker unknown**

*Pot of Flowers Quilt*

Probably Ohio

Mid 19th century

Appliquéd and quilted cotton

87" x 84"

Purchased from Florence Cowdin

Peto, 1955

10-165 (1955-644)

The quilt's pattern and colors are similar to about two dozen mid 19th-century quilts in private and museum collections that share the pot of flowers design. Five are dated 1854 to 1862, and nine came from families that have histories in Ohio. (See *One Pot of Flowers Quilt Pattern* by Connie J. Nordstrom, *Uncoverings,* Vol. 23, Research Papers of the American Quilt Study Group, 2002.)

**Attributed to Mary Beaman Cummings (1825-1904)**

*Lily Flower Quilt*
Princeton, Massachusetts
Mid 19th century
Inscribed on the back *No. 6 M.B.*
Pieced, appliquéd, and quilted
cotton
92" x 93"
Gift of Olive Lewis, 1994
10-732 (1994-2)

The quilt bears the inscription on its reverse *No. 6 M.B.*, which may mean that Mary Beaman owned (or, probably, made) at least six quilts before she married the Rev. Henry Cummings in 1851. No other quilts marked *M.B.* have yet been identified. During her husband's career as a Congregational minister, the couple and their five children lived in Newport, New Hampshire; Rutland, Massachusetts; and, by 1874, Strafford, Vermont. Mary Beaman's great-granddaughter gave the quilt to Shelburne Museum.

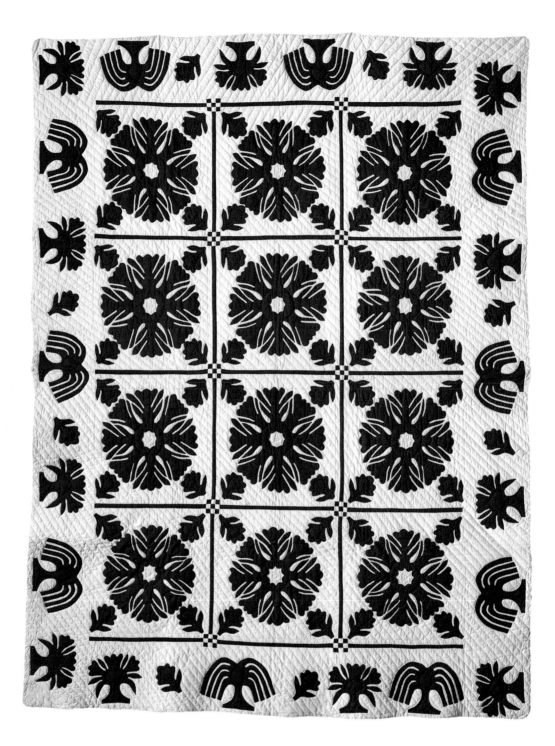

**Maker unknown**

*Snowflake and Willow Tree Quilt*

Probably Boston, Massachusetts

Mid 19th century

Appliquéd and quilted cotton

92" x 72"

Purchased from Margaret H.

Johnson, 1958

10-274 (1958-23)

The overall design of this quilt, with its abstract snowflake design and willow tree border, probably was inspired by the white and blue medallion patterns seen on English Jacquard-woven coverlets that were imported in the U.S. beginning in the early 19th century and later made here.

Margaret H. Johnson, from whom the Museum bought this quilt, thought it had been made in Boston.

**Carrie M. Carpenter
(b. 1835)**

*Sunflower Quilt*

Northfield, Vermont

Late 19th century

Inscribed in ink on the back *Carrie
M. Carpenter*

Appliquéd and quilted cotton

78" x 85"

Gift of Ethel Washburn, 1987

10-651 (1987-19)

The tall sunflowers appliquéd and quilted on this bedcover probably
were inspired by the mid 19th-century design vocabulary of the English
Arts and Crafts Movement, which was widely known in America through
books and magazines. The flowers, leaves, and stems were appliquéd
onto the white background, which is richly textured with hand-quilted
stitches. The maker inscribed her name on the back of the quilt: *Carrie
M. Carpenter*. In 1861, Miss Carpenter married William L. Smith, and
in 1888 their daughter Gertie married William H. Washburn. Their
daughter, Ethel Washburn, gave this quilt to the Museum in 1987.

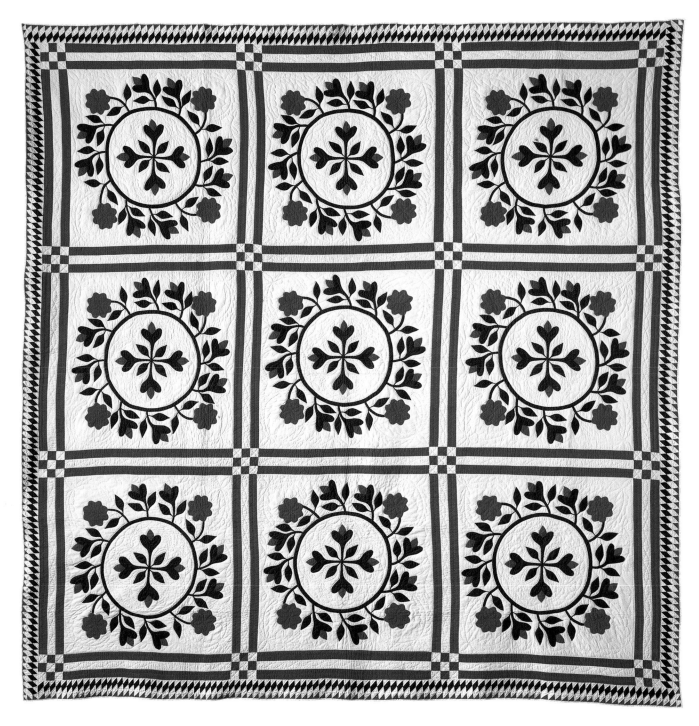

**Made by members of the Traver family**

*Presidential Wreath Quilt*

Sand Lake, New York

About 1845

Appliquéd and quilted cotton

96" x 96"

Museum purchase, 1979 with funds donated by Kitty Webb Harris

10-588 (1979-33)

The presidential wreath pattern is thought to have been inspired by Nathaniel Currier's 1845 print of George Washington's inaugural parade in 1789. The print is "Washington's Reception by the Ladies, On Passing the Bridge at Trenton, N.J. April 1789 On his Way to New York to be Inaugurated First President of the United States." It depicts women with rose wreaths in their hair strewing blossoms in front of Washington's procession along streets decorated with rose garlands.

**Mary Jane Terwilliger**

*Presidential Wreath Quilt*

New York

Stitched *1852 Mary Jane Terwilliger*

Appliquéd, embroidered, and

quilted cotton

91" x 73"

Museum purchase, 1960

10-381 (1960-127)

This pattern is a variant of the quilt opposite (page 62).

**Maker unknown**

*Virginia Lily*

Place of origin unknown

Mid 19th century

Pieced and appliquéd cotton

91½" x 89½"

Museum purchase, 1963

10-444 (1963-249.2)

**Maker unknown**

*Bias Pomegranate Quilt*

Place of origin unknown

Probably mid 19th century

Appliquéd and quilted cotton

88" x 86"

Museum purchase

10-321

**Mary A. Purdy**

*Feathered Star Quilt*

Springfield Center, New York

Signed bottom right *Mary A.*
*Purdy, June 12 1869*

Pieced and appliquéd cotton

91" x 82"

Museum purchase, 1959

10-349 (1959-162.5)

**Maker unknown**

*Basket of Flowers and Sawtooth*
*Triangle Quilt*

Place of origin unknown

Probably late 19th century

Appliquéd, pieced, and quilted
cotton

87³/4" x 76"

Gift of John Wilmerding, 2002

2002-25.1

**Maker unknown**

*Peacocks and Peahens Bedcover*

Place of origin unknown

Late 19th century

Appliquéd and embroidered
cotton; unquilted

104" x 100"

Gift of Electra Havemeyer Webb,
1952

10-90 (1952-611)

The rich decoration of this bedcover seems to be taken from the vocabulary of the Aesthetic Movement, a sophisticated design movement in the last quarter of the 19th century in both England and America. At that period there was a particular interest in exotic motifs, including peacocks. Note the use of layered fabrics to create subtle and original effects.

A famous example of an Aesthetic Movement interior is James McNeil Whistler's 1870s Peacock Room from London, now at the Smithsonian's Freer Art Gallery in Washington, D.C.

**Maker unknown**

*Oak Leaf and Orange Slice Bedcover*

Northeastern U.S.

Mid 19th century

Appliquéd cotton; unquilted

110" x 91½"

Gift of Richard Gipson and Roger
Wentworth, 1956

10-204 (1956-553)

Six different floral chintz fabrics in rich, glowing colors were used in
these blocks, and two additional prints were used for the sashes and
wide border. The oak leaf and orange slice patterns probably were made
by folding a square piece of paper into quarters and cutting out the
shape, which was then unfolded to reveal the design for a block.

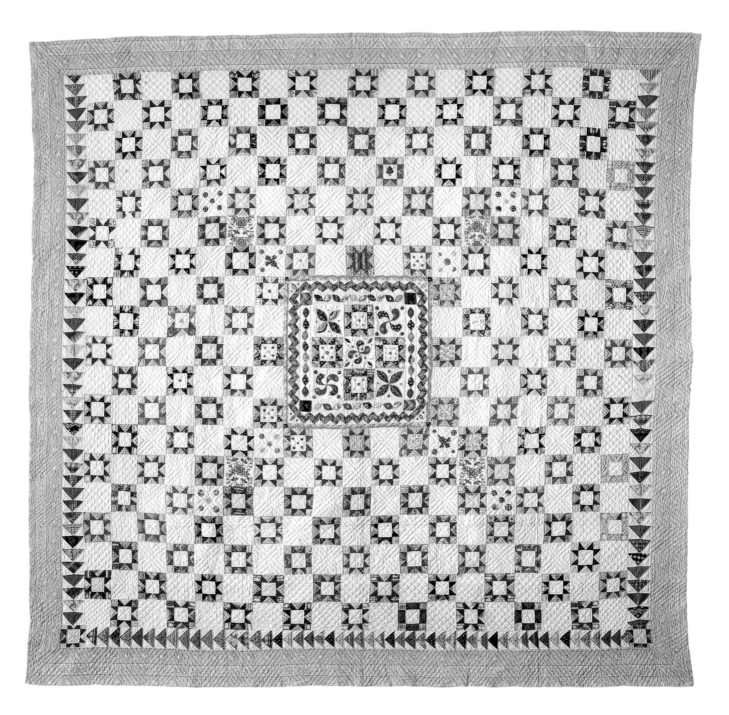

**Sarah Johnson
(1812-1876)**

*Stars and Pinwheel Medallion Quilt*
Pennsylvania
Inscribed in ink on the back *Sarah
Johnson No. 4 1826*
Pieced, appliquéd, and quilted
cotton
92" x 89"
Purchased from Elizabeth Spangler,
Ephrata, Pennsylvania, 1958
10-283 (1958-82.10)

Sarah Johnson was born in 1812 in Cochranville, Pennsylvania. She was 14 years old when she made this quilt, which has over 50 different printed fabrics. The *No. 4* inscription probably indicates that this was the fourth quilt Sarah made. In 1845, she married John Holcombe, and they lived in Lancaster County. Sarah, who had no children, left some of her quilts to her husband on her death. The Museum bought this quilt in 1958 from Mr. Holcombe's step-son's estate.

**Makers unknown**

*Oak Leaf Friendship Album Quilt*
54 names stitched or in ink,
including two of the Van Horn
family
New York
Mid 19th century
Appliquéd and quilted cotton
99" x 96"
Gift of J. Watson Webb Jr., 1974
10-556 (1974-001)

(not included in the exhibition)

**Maker unknown**

*Grapevine and Tulip Quilt*
New York
Mid 19th century
Appliquéd and quilted cotton
101" x 87"
Museum purchase, 1959
10-350 (1959-176)

**Maker unknown**

*Heart and Star Medallion Quilt*

New York

Mid 19th century

Appliquéd and quilted cotton

88" x 78"

Museum purchase, 1952

10-31 (1952-544)

The use of appliquéd hearts suggests that a bride may have made this quilt to celebrate her wedding. It was considered bad luck to use hearts except for marriage quilts. The lovers' knots on the border further emphasize the wedding symbolism; ribbon knots were often exchanged by couples and worn as a pledge of love and constancy.

**Maker unknown**

*Tulip and Orange Slice Quilt*

Kingston, Massachusetts

Mid 19th century

Pieced, appliquéd, and quilted

cotton

94" x 93"

Museum purchase, 1957

10-257 (1957-649.1)

The white ground is filled with quilted feathered scrolls, flower sprays, and a trailing grapevine. The quilt has an unusual scalloped edge trimmed in red. Note that the leaves in one corner block were made a different color as a deliberate imperfection. It is a manifestation of the superstition that the quilt-maker could avert misfortune by not competing with the gods to create a perfect thing.

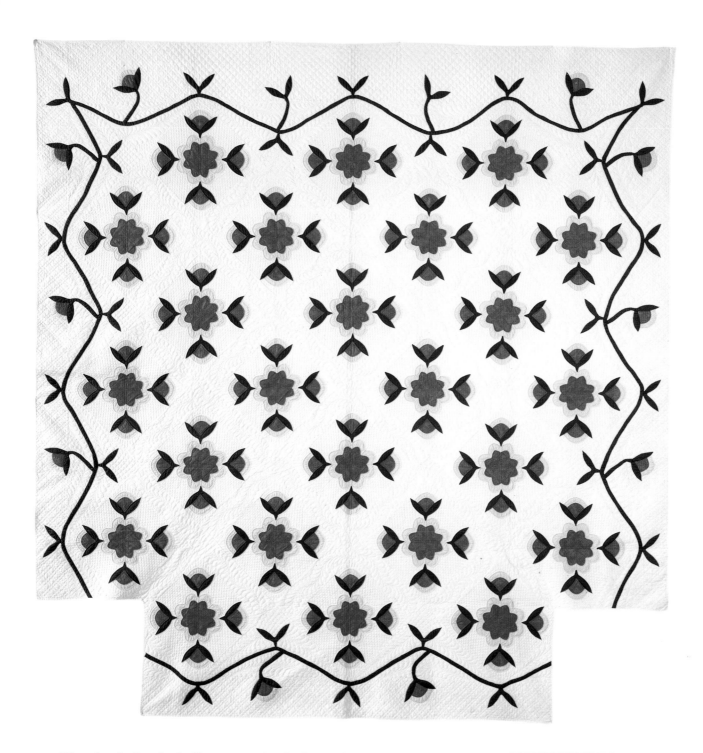

## Elizabeth Ruth Colburn (b. 1839)

*Rose and Bud Quilt*

Pittsford, Vermont

Mid 19th century

Signed on the back *E.R. Colburn*

Appliquéd and quilted cotton

92" x 88"

Gift of Mr. and Mrs. Robert E. Degenhardt, 1987

10-652 (1987-17)

Elizabeth Ruth Colburn was born on February 19, 1839, the eldest daughter of Horace (b. 1805) and Amaranth Smith (b. 1811) of Pittsford, Vermont. The signature *E.R. Colburn* on the reverse indicates that Elizabeth made this quilt before her first marriage, in 1861, to a Mr. Aldrich.

*Elizabeth Ruth Colburn, date unknown, Shelburne Museum archives, 27.12.2-27.*

**Maker unknown**

*Crossed Laurel Leaf Quilt*

Possibly Presque Isle, Maine

Mid 19th century

Appliquéd and quilted cotton

93" x 76"

Gift of Edith H. Porter, 1954

10-183 (1954-423)

Almost nothing is known for certain about this quilt's origins. Edith Porter, who gave it to the Museum in 1954, thought it had been made in Maine by the grandmother of a Mrs. S.S. Laird of Burlington, Vermont. When the Museum made inquiries, however, Mrs. Laird did not remember the quilt and knew only that her grandmother's name was Powers and that she had lived near Presque Isle, Maine. Such incomplete documentation is often the case in quilt histories.

**Olga Six Baker
(1899-1991)**

*Wind-Blown Tulips Quilt*

Detroit, Michigan

About 1930

87¹/₂" x 87¹/₂"

Appliquéd and quilted cotton

Gift of Olga Six Baker, 1991

10-711 (1991-39)

This pattern first appeared in *Ladies Home Journal* in 1911. It was later published by Marie Webster, an important figure in the promotion of American quilt-making in the early 20th century. In 1915, she brought out a book of designs, *Quilts: Their Story and How to Make Them*. The caption for this pattern read, "Seems to bring a breath of springtime both in form and color. Even the border flowers seem to be waving and nodding in the breeze."

Mrs. Baker, who made this example, was born in Illinois. She was a schoolteacher in Detroit when she worked on this quilt. In 1935, she and her husband moved to Baxter, Georgia, where she died in 1991.

Appliquéd Quilts

**Maker unknown**

*Foundation Rose Variation Quilt*

Northeastern U.S.

Mid 19th century

Appliquéd and quilted cotton

90" x 87"

Museum purchase, 1959

10-351 (1959-176)

After about 1840, the rising popularity of solid-colored (rather than chintz) appliqué quilts paralleled the availability and preference of cheaper printed cottons over the more expensive chintz fabrics. The predominant use of red and green in this quilt is an example of the influence of the Pennsylvania German community on quilt production.

**Attributed to a member of the Griswold family**

*Garden of Flowers, Fruits, and Birds Bedcover*

Connecticut

Marked center top *J.S.* and *1868*

Appliquéd cotton; unquilted

94" x 95"

Purchased from Florence Cowdin Peto, 1954

10-123 (1954-477.3)

Horticulturists will identify the emperor tulips, dahlias, fuchsias, pinks, roses, and carnations in this piece. Fruits include purple fox grapes, wild cherries (or china berries), and pears. The designs probably came from books published for the instruction of amateur artists.

Florence Cowdin Peto, from whom the Museum purchased this quilt, said it was made by a member of the Griswold family in Connecticut.

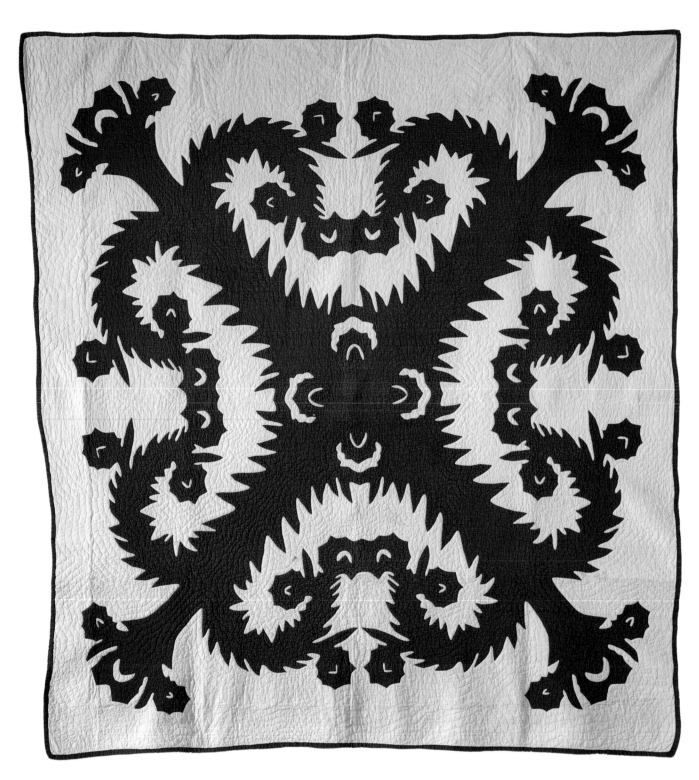

**Maker unknown**

*Hawaiian Quilt*

20th century

Hawaii

Appliquéd and quilted cotton

78¹/₂" x 75"

Museum purchase, 1973

10-550 (1973-35)

In Hawaii, this pattern is often known as *Na Wai O Maunaolu* (The Waters of Maunaolu). The literal translation is *cool mountain*. Maunaolu is an area on the island of Maui.

When New England missionaries first arrived in Hawaii in 1820, Hawaiians already had a long tradition of colored bedcovers called *kappa moe*. Quilts with a single large appliquéd fabric have been recorded since the 1870s.

**Ellen Fullard Wright
(1818–1889)**

*Lone Star Medallion Quilt*

Late 19th century

Rhode Island

Pieced, appliquéd, and quilted cotton

95" x 73"

Museum purchase, 1991

10-717 (1991-26)

The Museum acquired this quilt from Miriam Hoyt, great-granddaughter of the maker. Ellen Fullard was born in Bolton, Lancashire, England, and immigrated to America in 1842. By 1860, she and her husband, James Wright, were living in Rhode Island with their four children.

*Ellen Fullard Wright, date unknown, Shelburne Museum archives.*

# Pieced Quilts

Early 19th-century designs for pieced quilts often were copied from prototypes published in English periodicals. One of the first known publications of a pieced quilt pattern in the United States is for a hexagonal block that was illustrated in the January 1835 issue of *Godey's Lady's Book*. A magnificent example in Shelburne Museum's collection is *Hexagon Medallion Bedcover* (10-240), made about 1840 and attributed to Jane Morton Cook.

In an 1857 issue of *Godey's Lady's Book*, Ellen Lindsay wrote, "What little girl does not recollect her first of patchwork, the anxiety for fear the pieces would not fit, the eager care with which each stitch was taken, and the delight of finding the bright squares successfully blended into the pretty pattern?"

By mid-century, patterns for pieced (or patchwork) quilts were easy to find in women's periodicals, and they have remained popular among quilters to this day.

*Detail of Stenciled Flower, Leaf, and Bird Quilt (10-518), see page 100.*

**Attributed to Mary Canfield Benedict (1830-1920)**

*Mariner's Compass Quilt*

Arlington, Vermont

Mid 19th century

Pieced and quilted cotton

94" x 90"

Museum purchase, 1954

10-143 (1954-434)

When the Museum purchased the quilt in 1954, the Vermont seller said it had been made by Mary Canfield Benedict before her marriage to Fayette Shephard Baker of Arlington in 1852.

A mariner's compass consists of a magnetized pointer and a compass card, which is the movable circular dial divided into 32 equal points of the compass.

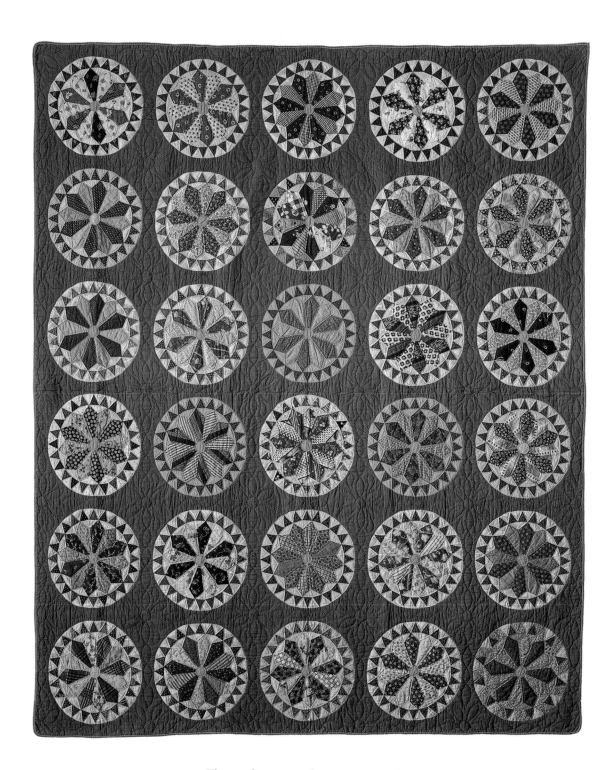

**Attributed to Emma Jane Perry Proctor**

*Pyrotechnic Star Quilt*

Fair Haven, Vermont

Mid 19th century

Pieced and quilted cotton

92" x 78"

Gift of Hazel Proctor Ibbotson, 1994

10-731 (1994-3)

This quilt came to the Museum with a note stating that it had been made by the donor's ancestor, Emma Proctor, of Fair Haven, Vermont. The quilt's pattern appears to be a modified mariner's compass design.

In 1935, quilt-makers and historians Carrie Hall and Rose Kretsinger documented hundreds of quilt patterns in their book, *The Romance of the Patchwork Quilt in America*. They included a pattern block almost identical to this, called pyrotechnics, which they described as "a very intricate and beautiful design not to be undertaken except by an experienced quilter."

**Maker unknown**

*Lesson in Geometry Quilt*

Place of origin unknown

Mid 19th century

Pieced and quilted cotton

93" x 78"

Museum purchase, 1959

10-334 (1959-27.2)

The artistic economy of using just two colors and a limited range of patterns make this a fine and unusual piece. The quilt shows little evidence of wear and retains some of the pencil lines that marked the pattern.

The lesson in geometry pattern is a variation of the economy patch design. Nothing about its origins is recorded.

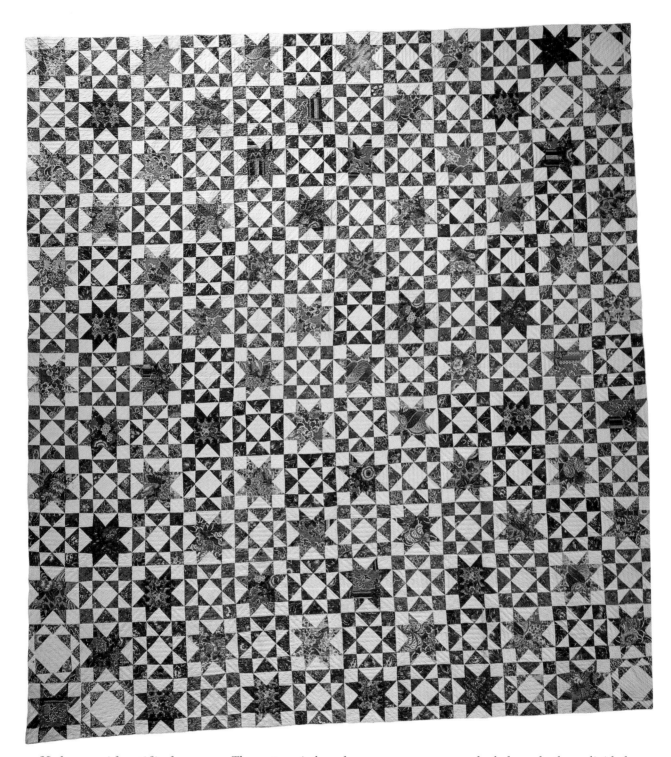

**Maker unidentified**

*Variable Star Pattern Quilt*

Pennsylvania

Cross-stitched on the back *ELH* and

*1839*

Pieced and quilted cotton

115" x 123"

Purchased from Elizabeth Spangler,

Ephrata, Pennsylvania, 1954

10-126 (1954-478.2)

The pattern is based on squares, some used whole and others divided into triangles. Five blocks are deliberately made in another pattern. It is said that some quilt makers believed that only God could achieve perfection and that it was presumptuous of mortals to try. Consequently, quilters sometimes incorporated a deliberate imperfection into their finished work.

Star quilts are made in innumerable variations, such as morning star, Ohio star, evening star, and Lemoyne star.

**Attributed to Jane Morton Cook**

*Hexagonal Medallion Bedcover*

Northeastern U.S.

About 1840

Cross-stitched on the lining in two places J$^C$M

Pieced cotton; unquilted

115" x 99"

Purchased from Mrs. Francis Hannigan, 1957

10-240 (1957-524)

The hexagon pattern was used extensively in England from the late 18th through the 19th century. An English example in Shelburne's collection (10-238) was made in 1835. That same year, an article in *Godey's Lady's Book*, published in Philadelphia, suggested that "there is not a patchwork that is prettier or more ingenious than the hexagon or six sided; this is also called the honey-comb patchwork."

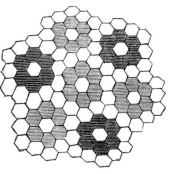

*Hexagon quilt pattern from* Godey's Lady's Book, *January 1835.*

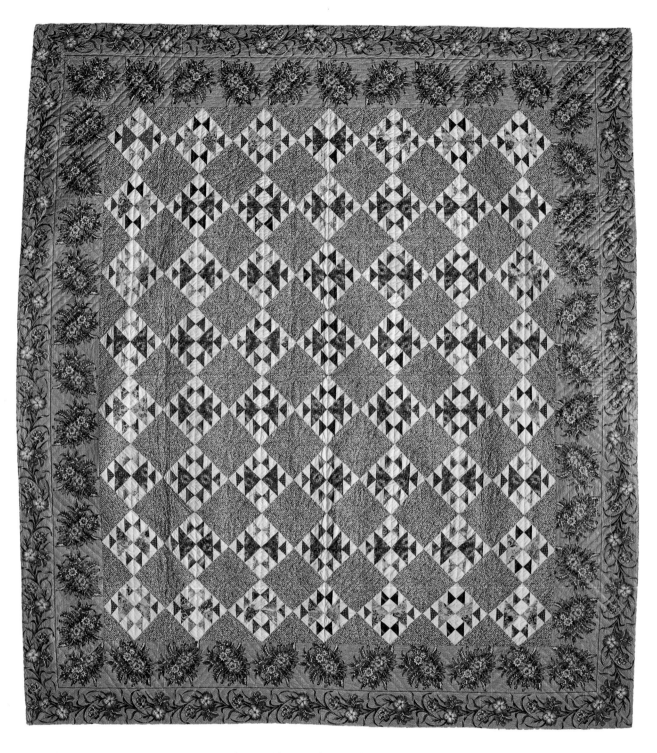

**Maker unknown**

*Geese and Foxes Quilt*

Probably Pennsylvania

Mid 19th century

Pieced and quilted cotton

97" x 87"

Purchased from Elizabeth

Spangler, Ephrata, Pennsylvania,

1955

10-192 (1955-701.12)

The small triangles in this quilt represent geese, and the larger ones, foxes. The fabric still has its glaze intact, indicating the quilt was never washed and, possibly, never used.

**Attributed to a member of the Vanderbilt family**

*Pincushion Quilt*

Probably New York

Mid 19th century

Pieced and quilted cotton

93" x 79"

Purchased from Florence Cowdin

Peto, 1955

10-164 (1955-676)

This piece is a fine example of a scrap quilt made from richly colored calicoes, ginghams, and chintzes. In Florence Cowdin Peto's book *American Quilts and Coverlets* (1949), she wrote that "it was made by a member of the Vanderbilt family in 1835" but offered no supporting evidence.

**Maker unknown**

*Eight-Point Stars Quilt*

Northeastern U.S.

Early 19th century

Pieced and quilted wool

86" x 105"

Museum acquisition

10-740

The quilt is made of medium-weight wool cloth and filled with carded raw wool. The red stars on the dark blue ground appear to float above the quilt's surface, while those within the beige diamonds anchor the overall pattern in a cohesive whole.

**Eunice Baker Willard**

*Sunburst and Sawtooth Quilt*

Castleton, Vermont

Mid 19th century

Pieced and quilted cotton

89" x 88½"

Museum purchase, 1954

10-166 (1954-454.1)

When the Museum acquired this quilt in 1954, an envelope pinned to it identified the maker as Eunice Baker Willard, who was born in 1823 in Pawlet, Vermont. Family tradition holds that she made the quilt about 1860 while she was living in nearby Castleton.

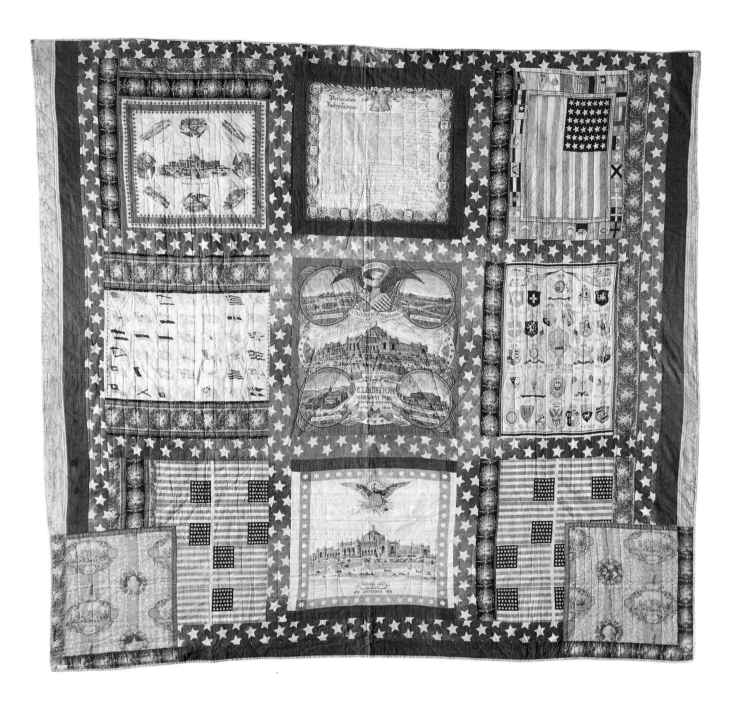

**Maker unknown**

*Centennial Exhibition Quilt*

Northeastern U.S.

About 1876

Pieced and quilted cotton

88" x 94"

Gift of J. Watson Webb, Jr., 1952

10-48 (1952-571)

The quilt's top is made from cotton printed with American flag stars and with souvenir handkerchiefs of the 1876 Philadelphia Centennial Exhibition, which commemorated the 100th anniversary of the Declaration of Independence. The center panel features Memorial Hall, the main building at the Exhibition. The stars on the quilt's reverse side are not pieced but the diamonds and large stars are.

*Detail from the reverse of 10-48*

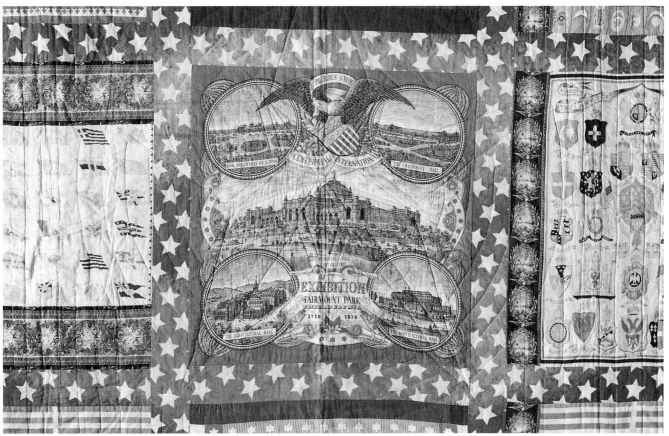

*Detail from the front of 10-48*

Pieced Quilts

**Maker unknown**

*Hexagons and Triangles Quilt*

Pennsylvania

Mid 19th century

Pieced and quilted cotton

97"x 76"

Museum acquisition

10-338

This idiosyncratic and bold pattern, dominated by red hexagons and yellow stripes, incorporates chintzes that have been pieced to create an undulating, kaleidoscopic background. It is a remarkable and original design.

**Maker unknown**

*Lone Star Quilt*

Ohio

1850-80

Pieced and quilted cotton

103" x 102"

Museum purchase, New York City,

1960

10-373 (1960-66.1)

For this spectacular quilt, the maker has created a dramatic kaleido-scopic effect using large and small white squares (with triangles and rectangles around the edges) quilted with monochromatic flower and fruit patterns. The shapes seem to float across the colorful pattern of concentric circles.

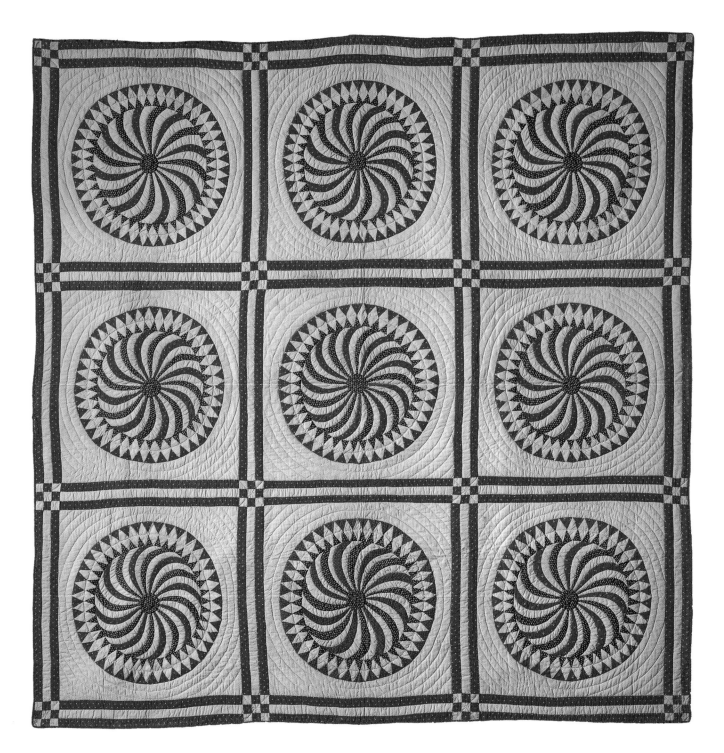

**Maker unknown**

*Nine Pinwheels Quilt*

Probably Long Island, New York

Mid 19th century

Pieced and quilted cotton

82" x 82"

Gift of Roger Wentworth, 1958

10-299 (1958-174)

This common pattern is more often seen with a greater number of smaller pinwheels, but by enlarging just nine pinwheels, it has been transformed into a dynamic and showy design.

The donor said that this quilt was from Long Island, New York.

**Maker unknown**

*Mariner's Compass Quilt*

Place of origin unknown

Mid 19th century

Pieced, appliquéd, and quilted

cotton

100" x 96"

Purchased from Florence Cowdin

Peto, 1952

10-22 (1952-545)

The mariner's compass pattern was used in English pieced quilts in the first half of the 18th century. Revivals of the design appeared in the 1889 *Ladies' Art Catalog* and other late 19th- and early 20th-century pattern books.

This example is of outstanding quality in both design and quality of needlework. A quilt of similar pattern and workmanship at the Museum of the City of New York is marked *Emeline Barker*.

**Maker unknown**

*Sunburst Star Quilt*

Pennsylvania

Late 19th century

Pieced and quilted wool and cotton

83" x 76"

Gift of John Wilmerding, 1997

10-771 (1997-28)

The sunburst pattern was common in the second half of the 19th century. The maker of this quilt used everyday scraps of printed and plaid cotton flannels, challis, and cretonnes (colorfully printed heavy cottons used for drapery and slipcovers).

**Unknown Sioux Indian maker**

*Bethlehem Star Quilt*
Probably North Dakota Plains
Late 19th or early 20th century
Pieced, appliquéd, and quilted
cotton
78" x 70"
Gift of John Wilmerding, 1988
10-658 (1988-16)

This quilt, the only one in Shelburne's collection made by a Native American, combines the Bethlehem star pattern with blocks of appliquéd flowers forming the border. The design is similar to those used in traditional Sioux beadwork.

All piecing and quilting in this bedcover was done by hand, and the narrow pink binding was sewn by machine.

**Maker unidentified**

*Stenciled Flower, Leaf, and Bird Quilt*

Place of origin unknown

Late 19th century

Stenciled in center *R.S.B.*

Pieced, painted, and quilted cotton

89" x 89"

Museum purchase, 1969

10-518 (1969-53)

The blue-gray color was sprayed over flowers, fern leafs, and bird stencils to look like early 19th-century photographic images produced on sensitized paper. Hatched lines to define stamens and feathers were drawn free-hand. Over 4,000 small white and red triangles were pieced to create the finished quilt, which is an extraordinary piece.

**Made by Meacham family members and friends**

*Friendship Quilt*

New York

Mid 19th century

Pieced and quilted cotton

82" x 77"

Gift of Agnes K. Lovell, 1975

10-573 (1975-55)

This double-sashed diamond quilt was given to the Museum by a descendant of its original owner, Dorcas Eliza Meacham. She is said to have received the piece as a wedding present in the 1860s, when she lived near Ithaca, New York. Among the signatures on the quilt are several with the last name of Meacham, Leach, Pierce, and Hurlburt. Although somewhat faded, the quilt still makes a vivid impression.

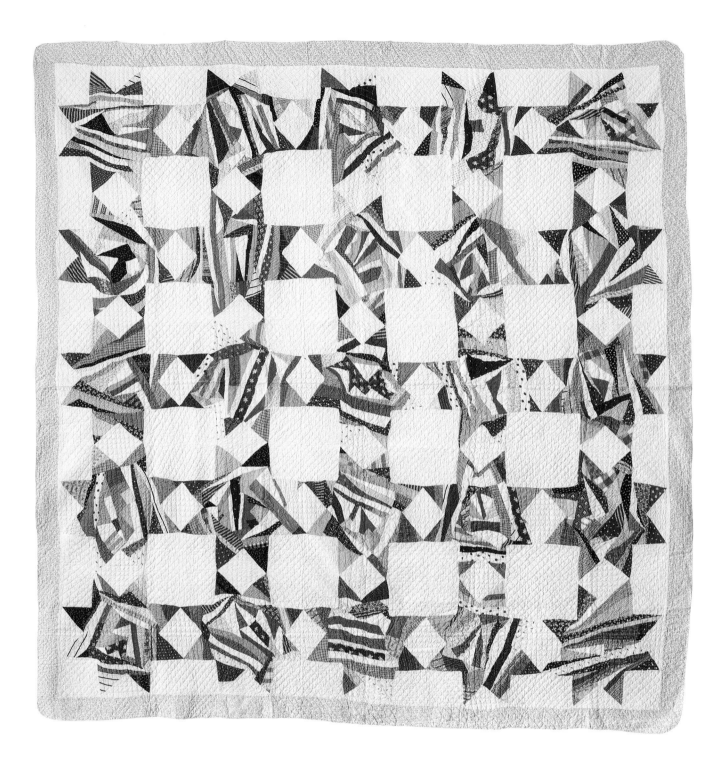

**Maker unknown**

*Crazy Star Quilt*

Place of origin unknown

Late 19th or early 20th century

Pieced and quilted cotton

86" x 81"

Museum purchase, 1990

10-708 (1990-44)

The pattern is a variant of both the star and crazy quilt styles. The quilt's interesting design and splendidly chosen fabrics create a lively and colorful effect. Crazy quilts often were made for display rather than to be used, but the maker of this quilt clearly had function in mind when she chose durable cotton fabrics. It is filled with cotton batting and backed with soft cotton.

**Maker unknown**

*Cross-Stitch Quilt*

Ballston Spa, New York

Late 19th century

Pieced and quilted cotton

89" x 87"

Museum purchase, 1996

10-754 (1996-14)

This quilt was found in the mid 1990s in an attic trunk in a house in the Ballston Spa area of New York. No documentation about its origins have come to light, but the design of the African American figures is based on small-scale embroidery patterns published in the late 19th century. Here, they have been greatly enlarged to suit the size of the quilt.

**Maker unknown**
*Puritan Star Crib Quilt*
Probably Connecticut
Late 19th century
Pieced and quilted cotton
34½" x 27"
Museum purchase, 1961
10-406 (1961-102)

**Maker unknown**
*Lemoyne Star and Sawtooth Star
Crib Quilt*
Probably Pennsylvania
Mid 19th century
Pieced and quilted cotton
39" x 39"
Gift of Elizabeth Spangler,
Ephrata, Pennsylvania, 1957
10-285 (1957-565)

**Caroline Treff Witt
(b. 1865?)**

*Floral Album Quilt*

Leavenworth, Kansas

1930s

Pieced, appliquéd, and quilted

cotton

84" x 69"

Gift of Wayne Schiffelbein, 1997

10-778 (1997-44.5)

This is one of the best 20th-century quilts in the Museum's collection. Its colors are typical of the period, and its overall design is distinctive of the colonial revival style. Note the charmingly arranged flowers and the scalloped edge. Caroline Witt probably found the pattern in a women's magazine.

**Josephine Mary Carpenter (1851-1912)**

*Log Cabin (Windmill Blades) Quilt*

About 1900

East Charlotte, Vermont

Pieced and quilted cotton and wool

83" x 68"

Purchased from Mrs. Henry Cole, 1954

10-133 (1954-421)

Because of the sense of movement created by ingeniously arranged light and dark strips, this is perhaps the Museum's best log cabin quilt. Josephine Mary Cushman was born in Middlebury, Vermont, and she married Joseph Carpenter (b. 1845) in 1867. They farmed in East Charlotte, just south of Shelburne.

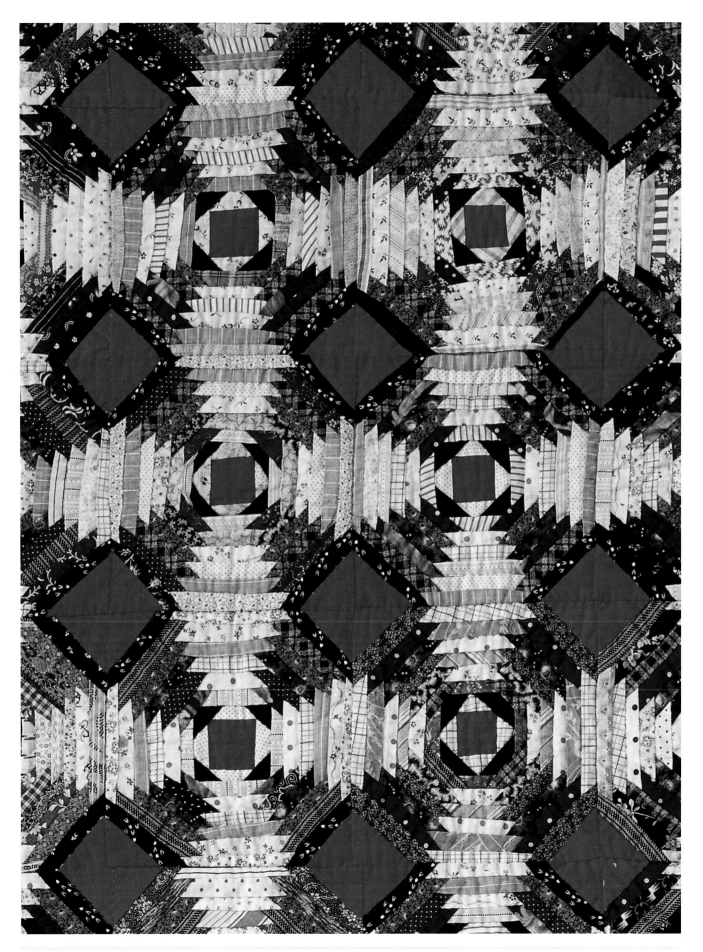

**Maker unknown**

*Log Cabin Quilt Top*

Massachusetts

Late 19th century

Pieced silk; unquilted

65" x 65"

Gift of Esther M. Dunning, 1970

10-527 (1970-96)

The maker used a variety of silk satins and velvets to create a dramatic and refined kaleidoscope effect. The piece was never finished; its edges have not been bound, and it is not quilted. It has, therefore, never been used and is in mint condition.

**Maker unknown**

*Log Cabin Barn-Raising Quilt Top*

Place of origin unknown

Late 19th century

Pieced cotton and silk; unquilted

72" x 72"

Gift of Electra Havemeyer Webb,

1952

10-11 (1952-534)

**Jennie Sargent Green
(1851-1924)**

*Log Cabin Barn-Raising Quilt*

Rutland, Vermont

Late 19th century

Pieced and quilted cotton and

wool

79" x 78¹/₂"

Gift of Geneva Tetu, 1989

10-691 (1989-35)

**Bethia Willey Poor
(1820-1894)**

*Log Cabin Barn-Raising Quilt*

Williamstown, Vermont

1870-75

Pieced and quilted cotton

71" x 71"

Gift of Mrs. J.S. Hockenberry, 1970

10-533 (1970-125)

This is an excellent example of a log cabin quilt. Mrs. J.S. Hockenberry, who gave the quilt to the Museum, noted that it had been made by her grandmother, Bethia Willey Poor, either for the wedding of her son Edward (b. 1850) in 1872 or her daughter Mary (b. 1843) in 1875.

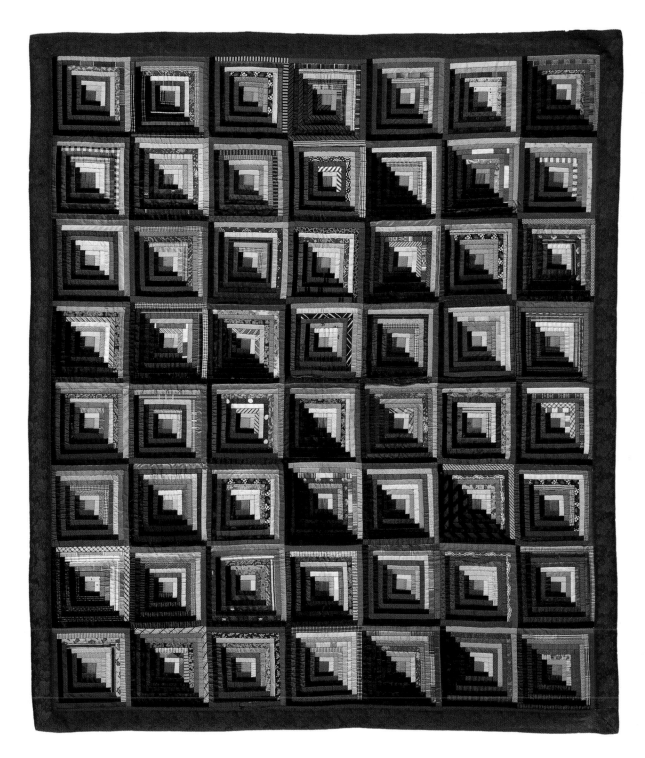

**Attributed to Sarah Furman or Jane Furman Allen**

*Straight-Furrow Log Cabin Quilt*

Rockland County, New York

Late 19th century

Pieced and tied silk

67¹/₂" x 58¹/₂"

Gift of Mrs. Carl Johnson, 1973

10-552 (1973-74)

The silk ribbons were carefully chosen to emphasize the strong lights and darks required to carry out the overall pattern. The resulting illusionistic effect emulates the receding sections of a coffered neoclassical ceiling.

Mrs. Carl Johnson, who gave the quilt to the Museum, said that it was made in West New Hampstead, Rockland County, New York either by her grandfather's grandmother, Sarah Furman, or her grandfather's mother, Jane Furman Allen.

**Ida W. Beck
(1880-1967)**

*Alphabet Monogram Quilt*

1950-1954

Easton, Pennsylvania

Embroidered and quilted cotton

94" x 90"

Gift of the maker, 1955

10-254 (1955-612)

In 1955 Miss Ida Beck wrote the Shelburne Museum describing her embroidered quilt. "It is hand quilted... quite original and I was several years in planning and making it. [I] am over 70 years old—a shut-in since childhood, so have always done needlework. And monogramming was my specialty for many years."

On the center panel is an alphabet monogram, and seven other alphabets in script, block, old English, and others. In all there are about 400 letters, all hand-embroidered in assorted colors, and about 50 flowers, each different.

**Maker unknown**

*Crazy Quilt*

Place of origin unknown

Late 19th century

Pieced silk and lace

66" x 65"

Gift of Mr. and Mrs. Peter Paine,
1981

10-597 (1981-53)

**Maker unknown**

*Flying Geese Quilt*

Vermont

Late 19th century

Pieced and tied silk

64" x 54"

Gift of Mrs. W.G.Wescott, 1959

10-354 (1959-161)

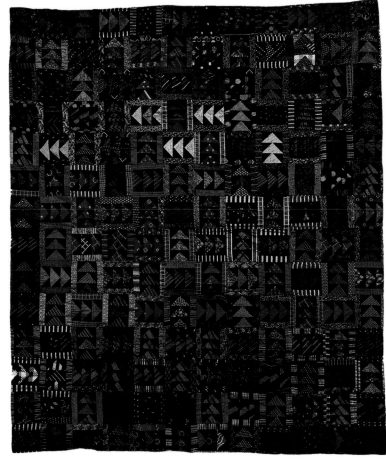

# Amish and Mennonite Quilts

Mennonites are descended from 16th-century Swiss Anabaptists, so named because of their belief in adult baptism or re-baptism. The term *Mennonite* was given the Anabaptists after a prominent leader, Menno Simons. In the 1690s, the Amish (led by Jacob Amman) broke from the Swiss Mennonite Church. The group migrated to Germany, and because of persecution there in 1727, to Lancaster County, Pennsylvania (at the invitation of William Penn). Later, they settled in other parts of Pennsylvania and in Ohio, Indiana, Kansas, and Iowa.

Today, the Amish still shun the worldly life and do not have such modern conveniences as cars, electricity, indoor plumbing, telephones, television, or computers. Amish women use treadle-powered sewing machines, and they make quilts from the same solid, sometimes brilliantly hued, cotton and wool fabrics that they use for their clothing.

The earliest Amish quilts date from the 1860s and feature large geometric forms made in bold, solid colors decorated with quilting. Amish quilting designs, especially scrolling feather patterns, are strongly reminiscent of late 18th- and early 19th-century English and American quilts. Later 19th-century Amish-made quilts contrast dramatically with those of their Anglo-American neighbors, who used more modern quilting styles.

*Detail of Concentric Squares Quilt (10-671), see page 119.*

**Unknown Amish maker**

*Double Nine-Patch Quilt*

Probably Indiana or Ohio

Early 20th century

Pieced and quilted cotton

85" x 83"

Purchased from Elaine Hart, New York City, 1989

10-667 (1989-52.2)

The pattern of nine diamonds inside a larger patch is a traditional Anglo-American design adopted by the Amish and made distinctively theirs by the use of colors that are restrained and yet visually striking. In this quilt, the small pink centers of each block catch the eye and are held in balance by the surrounding blues, reds, and greens. The hand-quilted feather wreaths in the large maroon squares echo the feather scrolls of the wide green border.

**Unknown Amish maker**
*Abstract Diamond Crib Quilt*
Kansas
Probably early 20th century
Pieced and quilted cotton
55" x 49"
Purchased from Elaine Hart, New
York City, 1988
10-677 (1988-52.12)

**Unknown Amish maker**
*Center Diamond in a Square Quilt*
Lancaster County, Pennsylvania
Early 20th century
Pieced and quilted wool
83" x 82"
Museum purchase, 1966
10-492 (1966-71)

**Unknown Amish maker**
*Center Diamond in a Square Quilt*
Lancaster County, Pennsylvania
Late 19th or early 20th century
Pieced and quilted wool
77" x 76"
Purchased from Elaine Hart, New
York City, 1989
10-666 (1989-52.1)

Among the Pennsylvania Amish, the center diamond in a square pattern is unique to Lancaster County, where the Amish first settled in the 1720s. Quilting in Lancaster County is considered to be the finest by Amish women anywhere.

In this piece, the exquisite needlework includes a seven-point central star, scrolling flowers (including tulips), and a border of feather scrolls. Wide outside borders and large corner blocks are typical of Amish designs, as is the wide binding.

**Unknown Amish maker**

*Concentric Squares Quilt*

Lancaster County, Pennsylvania

Early 20th century

Pieced and quilted wool

80" x 80"

Purchased from Elaine Hart, New
York City, 1989

10-671 (1989-52.6)

The alternating three red and three slate blue squares seem to pulsate
as they interact with each other, creating an extraordinary visual effect.
The red areas are beautifully quilted with diamonds, and the slate blue
with cables.

**Unknown Pennsylvania
German maker**

*Orange Basket Quilt*

Pennsylvania

Late 19th century

Pieced, appliquéd, and quilted cotton

83" x 72¹/₂"

Museum purchase, 1988

10-663 (1988-38)

Combinations of pink, green, and yellow are documented in a group of quilts made in Adams County, Pennsylvania in the late 19th century. Many of these quilts were worked by women of German and Dutch ancestry.

Bold green and yellow sashing emphasizes the orange basket pattern worked on a printed pink and red cotton background. The oranges are heavily stuffed so they appear in high relief.

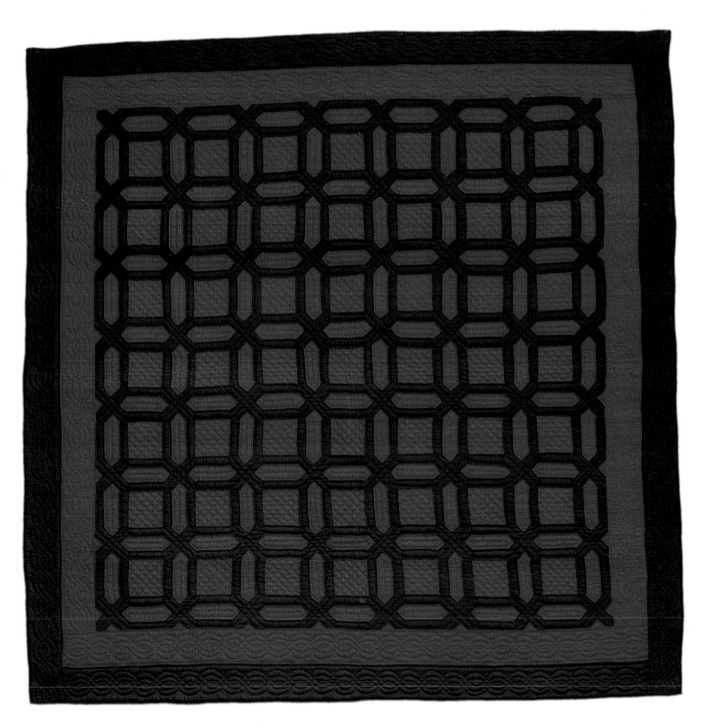

**Unknown Mennonite maker**
*Garden Maze Quilt*
Lancaster County, Pennsylvania
Late 19th or early 20th century
Pieced and quilted wool
80" x 79"
Purchased from Elaine Hart, New York City, 1988
10-669 (1988-52.4)

The garden maze pattern is created by the use of elaborate sashing. In this quilt, two rows of sashing connect to neighboring blocks to form interlocking hexagons. The inside squares are quilted with a diamond design. The quilt is more thickly padded than most 19th-century quilts.

# Crazy Patchwork Quilts

The making of crazy quilts, which have asymetrical patchwork designs of many different fabrics, became widespread in the 1880s and '90s. Articles about women cutting the linings out of men's coats and hats became ubiquitous in magazines, including *Godey's Ladies Book* and *Harper's Bazaar*. By the mid-1880s, enterprising manufacturers recognized the popularity of crazy quilts and began packaging remnants of satin, brocade, velvet, and other richly woven fabrics as ready-to-sew kits. Pre-cut fabric in crazy shapes could be bought with the design marked on a backing cloth for easy assembly. Some had embroidery designs stamped on them, including iron-on transfer patterns and oil-painted pictures for pressing onto fabric.

*Detail of Crazy Patchwork Quilt (2003-2), see page 126.*

**Delphia Noice Haskins
(1816-1892) or her
daughter, Ada Haskins
Pierce (b. 1848)**

*Crazy Patchwork Quilt*

Rochester, Vermont

1870-80

Pieced and appliquéd cotton

82" x 69"

Museum purchase, 1956

10-215 (1956-648)

The Museum has owned this quilt since 1956. In 2003, Henry Haskins Pierce, Jr., grandson of Ada Haskins, gave Shelburne another quilt (see page 126) by the same maker. A third, related quilt is privately owned (illustrated on page 127). Family history holds that the three quilts were made either by Delphia Haskins or her daughter Ada.

The quilter has used considerable imaginative freedom to create images that are striking in their liveliness.

**Delphia Noice Haskins (1816-1892) or her daughter, Ada Haskins Pierce (b. 1848)**

*Crazy Patchwork Quilt*

Rochester, Vermont

1888

Pieced and appliquéd cotton

91½" x 83"

Gift of Henry Haskins Pierce, Jr.,

2003

2003-2

Henry Haskins Pierce, Jr., a descendent of the maker, gave the quilt to Shelburne Museum in 2003. Family history holds that this quilt and two very similar to it were made either by Delphia Haskins or her daughter Ada, the donor's grandmother.

The two men's faces near the top are Benjamin Harrison and Levi Morton. Harrison served as president from 1889-1893 with Morton as his vice-president. The images were most likely cut from a printed handkerchief, which were commonly used during political campaigns of the late 19th century. The quilt can therefore be dated to the election year of 1888.

**Delphia Noice Haskins
(1816-1892) or her
daughter, Ada Haskins
Pierce (b. 1848)**

*Crazy Patchwork Quilt*

Private Collection

**Made by a member of the Eddy family**

*Crazy Patchwork Quilt*

New York

Stitched *1884* and *CAJ*

Pieced and embroidered silk

72" x 66"

Gift of Lenoir Eddy, 1997

10-766 (1997-22)

This quilt includes scraps of many different expensive and luxurious silks. Among the embroidered details are pansies, butterflies, the moon, and stars. Many of these scraps would have been marketed expressly for use in a crazy quilt.

**Catherine Mary Severance Winchester (1821-1915)**

*Crazy Patchwork Quilt*
New England
Late 19th century
Pieced and painted silk velvet and satin
71½" x 72"
Gift of Alice Winchester, 1992
10-719 (1992-36)

Catherine Winchester (born in Middlebury, Vermont) was both a needlewoman and a painter. This quilt was a gift to the Museum from her daughter Alice, who was the influential and well-known editor of *The Magazine Antiques* between 1938 and 1972. Alice Winchester encouraged and advised Electra Havemeyer Webb as the Shelburne Museum founder formed the quilt collection in the 1950s.

*Catherine Winchester, aged 92, in 1913.*

**Jeanette Brooks
Spaulding Wright
(b. 1834)**

*Crazy Patchwork Quilt*

Indianapolis, Indiana

Embroidered *Sept 5 1894*

Pieced and embroidered silk and
cotton

74" x 55"

Gift of Jeanette Sharp Andrus, 1984

10-618.1 (1984-54)

The quilt was a gift to the Museum by Jeanette Andrus, granddaughter of maker Jeanette Brooks Spaulding Wright. It was made for the marriage of Jeanette's daughter (and the donor's mother) Nettie in 1894.

Twelve blocks were made separately, then pieced together. There are painted and embroidered flowers and figures, including one based on the work of English children's book illustrator Kate Greenway. The quilt's ruffled border is made of velvet.

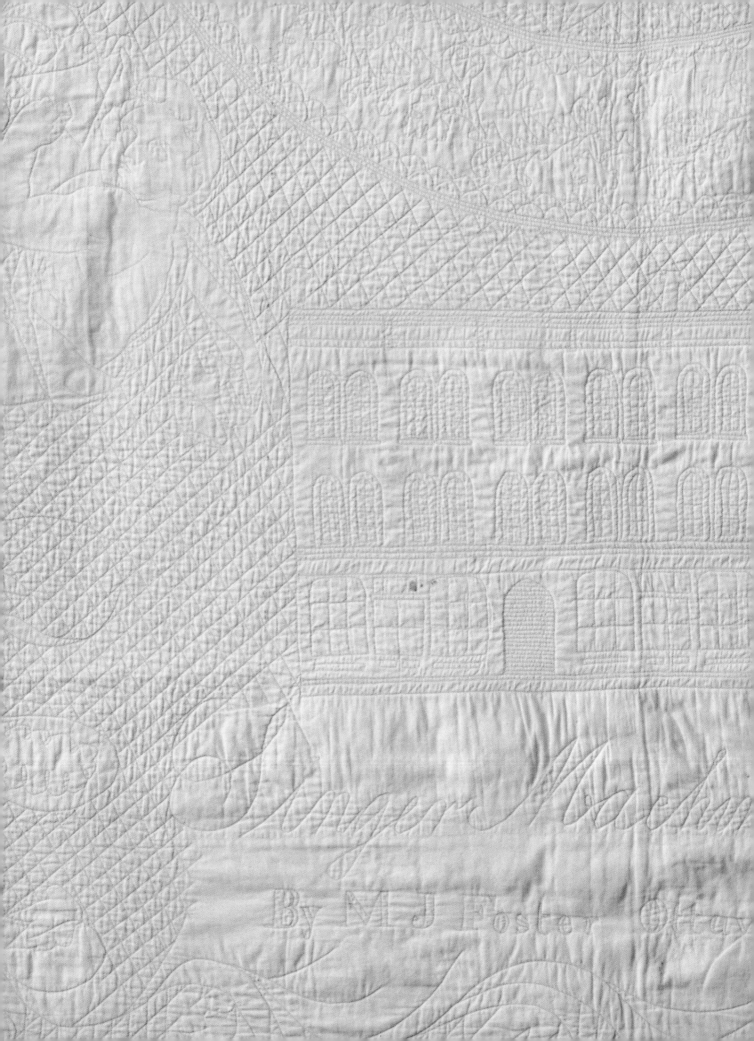

By M J Foster 64

# Whitework Quilts

Whitework quilts were made in the 18th century and were popular in the early 19th century, when the neoclassical style prevailed. They were highly prized and often were included in a bride's trousseau. The fashion was revived in the mid 19th century, perhaps because of the increased availability of factory-woven white cotton fabric and improved technology for washing.

Whitework quilts stitched by hand are the product of extremely skilled needleworkers. With no colors to help create a pattern, white stitches on a white ground demand an exacting eye, excellent technique, and extreme patience. Some of these examples use stuffed work, in which parts of a quilted design are stuffed from the back with soft cotton to give deep relief on the finished front.

*Detail of Singer Machine Work Whitework Quilt (10-405), see page 136.*

**Cornelia Thompson Noyes (1831-1862)**

*Double Medallion Whitework Quilt*

Buffalo, New York

Mid 19th century

Quilted cotton

99" x 83"

Museum gift, 1958

10-305 (1958-212)

When Cornelia Thompson Noyes died in 1862, her husband Daniel returned this quilt to the Thompson family, whose descendents in turn gave it to the Museum.

The stuffed work on this quilt is of exquisite quality.

**Maker unknown**

*Floral Wreath Whitework Quilt*

Probably Pennsylvania

Mid 19th century

Quilted cotton

104" x 92"

Purchased from Florence Cowdin

Peto, 1952

10-43 (1952-566)

This quilt is extremely well made and is in excellent condition. When the Museum bought it from quilt specialist Florence Peto, she suggested that it was from New Hope, Pennsylvania and that it was made about 1830.

**M.J. Foster**

*Singer Machine Work Whitework Quilt*

Ottawa, Illinois

Late 19th century

Stitched *Singer Sewing Machine*

*Work/By M J Foster Ottawa Illinois*

Machine-quilted cotton

82" x 81"

Museum purchase, 1961

10-405 (1961-98)

The quilt is unusual because it was quilted on a sewing machine at a time when, after the Civil War, most quilts were still made by hand despite the wider availability of machines. Only on some pieced work might a machine be used, and even then the quilting was usually by hand. On this quilt, a ***tour de force*** of machine work, are buildings, doves, eagles, a ship, a cherub, and flags.

**Unknown maker**

*Marseilles Quilt*

19th century

Machine-quilted cotton

108" x 108"

Museum purchase, 1958

10-284 (1958-82.12)

"Marseilles" quilting is the name given to yardage for use in clothing and bedcovers that were made in England, generally in the Manchester area, throughout most of the 19th century. In the 1880s home decorating manuals recommended Marseilles quilts for secondary bedrooms.

**Maker unknown**

*Sailing Ships Whitework Quilt*

Probably coastal New England

About 1850

Pieced, appliquéd, and stuff-worked

cotton

89" x 78"

Gift of Electra Havemeyer Webb,

1952

10-021 (1952-544)

The visual focus in this quilt is the stuff-worked designs of ships, compasses, and flowers. Sloop-rigged sailing vessels rest on undulating quilted lines representing waves while gulls soar in the white muslin sky.

# Selected Bibliography

Brackman, Barbara. *Encyclopedia of Pieced Quilt Patterns.* Paducah, Kentucky: American Quilter's Society, 1993.

Carlisle, Lilian Baker. *Pieced Work and Applique Quilts at Shelburne Museum.* Shelburne, Vermont: The Shelburne Museum, 1957.

Cord, Xenia. "Marketing Quilt Kits in the 1920s and 1930s," in *Uncoverings* 16 (1995): 139-173. San Francisco: American Quilt Study Group, 1995.

Goldsborough, Jennifer. *Lavish Legacies: Baltimore Album Quilts in the Collection of the Maryland Historical Society.* Baltimore, Maryland: MHS Press.

Granick, Eve Wheatcroft. *The Amish Quilt.* Intercourse, Pennsylvania: Good Books, 1989.

Fox, Sandi. *Small Endearments: Nineteenth-Century Quilts for Children and Dolls.* Nashville, Tennessee: Rutledge Hill Press, 1994 (2nd ed.).

Gunn, Virginia. "Crazy Quilts and Outline Quilts: Popular Responses to the Decorative Art/Art Needlework Movement, 1876-1893," in *Uncoverings* 5 (1984): 131-152. Mill Valley, California: American Quilt Study Group, 1985.

Irwin, John and Katharine B. Brett. *Origins of Chintz.* London: Her Majesty's Stationery Office, 1970.

Kobayashi, Kei, ed. *The Quilt.* Tokyo: Gakken Co., Ltd., 1985.

Montgomery, Florence M. *Printed Textiles: English and American Cottons and Linens 1700-1850.* New York: The Viking Press, 1970.

Nordstrom, Connie J. "One Pot of Flowers Quilt Pattern — Blossoming Through Centuries," in *Uncoverings* 23 (2002): 31-64. Lincoln, Nebraska: American Quilt Study Group, 2002.

Oliver, Celia, ed. *55 Famous Quilts from the Shelburne Museum.* New York: Dover Publications, Inc., 1990.

Oliver, Celia, ed. *Enduring Grace, Quilts from the Shelburne Museum Collection.* Lafayette, California: C&T Publishing, 1997.

Peck, Amelia. *American Quilts and Coverlets in the Metropolitan Museum of Art.* New York: Dutton Studio Books, 1990.

Pellman, Rachel and Kenneth. *The World of Amish Quilts.* Intercourse, Pennsylvania: Good Books, 1984.

*Quilts from the Shelburne Museum.* Tokyo: Kokusai Art, 1996.

Safford, Carleton L. and Robert Bishop. *America's Quilts and Coverlets.* New York: E.P. Dutton & Co., Inc., 1972.

Shaw, Robert. *Hawaiian Quilt Masterpieces.* New York: Hugh Lauter Levin Associates, Inc., 1996.

Webster, Marie D. *Quilts: Their Story and How to Make Them.* New York: Tudor Publishing Company, 1915.

# Index of Quilt Makers